In Pursuit Of
TROUT

In Pursuit Of
TROUT

EDITED BY BOB SOUTH

The
Halcyon
Press

Published by
The Halcyon Press.
A division of
Halcyon Publishing Ltd.
P.O. Box 360, Auckland 1015, New Zealand.

Printed in China
by
Prolong Press Limited

ISBN 1-877256-48-x
Copyright © 2005 Fairfax Publishing Ltd
First Published 2005
All Rights Reserved

Cover Photo: David Hallett
Back Cover Photo: David Hallett

Contents

People often ask me why I enjoy fishing, and I cannot explain it to them because there is no reason in the way they want meanings described. They are asking a man why he enjoys breathing when he really has no choice but to wonder at its truth...

Life is a greater challenge than death, and reality is as close as the nearest river.

A J MᶜCLANE

Introduction

BY BOB SOUTH

For 13 years now, *Fish & Game New Zealand* magazine has been arguably the country's leading flyfishing and bird hunting magazine. Audited readership figures alone indicate our position is at the tip of the flyrod, not near the butt section or reel seat. More than 200,000 readers can't be wrong. Awards suggest we are doing things right too. The magazine has consistently featured in national media awards, including winning the prestigious Qantas Media Awards Magazine of the Year (Special Interest) in 1996 and the equally important Magazine Publishers Association Awards for Magazine of the Year (Special Interest) in 2002.

We are indebted to those avid readers who have joined us on our journey over the years and our gratitude comes in the fashion of this very book, the second in our Fish & Game New Zealand Collection series. A great percentage of our followers are dedicated flyfishermen and women. This is not to ignore the bird shooters out there among our readers, sorry, nor the people who passionately combine both fishing and hunting as their sports. It is simply to say that this book is directed at those who compulsively enjoy trout and salmon and the pursuit thereof. This book is for people who want to get better at catching fish.

Already earlier this year, we started the Collection series with the book *Bird Hunting*, which was released in March as a prelude to yet another waterfowl and gamebird season. This is the flyfishing version — a compilation of some of the best how-to features on flyfishing that we have run in Fish & Game over the last 71 issues.

If one were to count the number of pages *Fish & Game New Zealand* has produced since its inception in 1993, that total would exceed 7000 pages. Much of it has been important and invaluable reading, not least the how-to advice from an extraordinary collection of contributors. We therefore think it is important to bind under one cover some of the best material from some of the finest freshwater fishing writers this country has on offer — now or ever. Repetition in many facets of life is often considered a weakness, a classic example of a lack of originality. But any indulgence in flyfishing depends... no thrives... on repetition: the cast, flytying, mending, stalking, and, yes, even reading the sport's plethora of literature. *Fish & Game New Zealand*, then, offers no excuses for reproducing what many of you may already have read. It is worth re-publishing. It is exceptional material, will always be applicable, and, now that so many quality features have been captured under one umbrella, this book threatens to become a "bible of sorts" on New Zealand flyfishing as much as any other yet produced.

Among those whose advice you will enjoy within these pages are premier guides Tony Entwistle, Jack MacKenzie, Zane Mirfin, and Peter Church, fisheries scientists Roger Young and John Hayes, rod design and casting expert Mark Sherburn, top fishermen as well as fisheries managers Ross Millichamp and Glenn Maclean, and angling officianados David Moate and Les Hill. A finer collection of expert angler/writers would be hard to find anywhere in the world. They cover topics as diverse as understanding flylines, correcting the casual cast, making pocket water productive, capturing fish in fast water, fishing the guts for salmon, perfecting perfect drift, catch and release, harling, trolling, jigging, small boat tactics, mastering difficult trout, nymphing and downstream fishing.

Our magazine came from small beginnings, certainly small enough to never think we might one day publish a Best Of series. But here we are and what a treat it is to be sharing this with you. My only hope is that you will glean as much meaningful information from our correspondents as I personally have.

BOB SOUTH

EDITOR

FISH & GAME NEW ZEALAND

Stacking The Odds Against The Fish

BY LES HILL

My brother and I earned pocket money in our youth thinning turnips for farmers during our school holidays along the banks of the Clutha River. After several hours toil in the fields, we welcomed the midday break and always raced to the riverbank and disappeared into the shade of the overhanging willows.

Other workers probably pictured us relaxing, eating our lunches. Instead, our sandwiches were wolfed down — the hour ahead was too precious to waste.

Along the willow-infested reaches, the flow of the river was negligible. The environment created by the willows was one of pockets of still, deep water — ideal for shoals of fat perch and the occasional cruising trout. Our lunch breaks were a time of pursuit, sneaking from pocket to pocket searching for feeding fish, and of patience when traps were set.

The most enduring memory of these days was the gear we used. We were armed as we worked in the field. Each with a 9ft roll of nylon, a single hook, and a small piece of lead in our pocket — nothing more. At the river's edge we attached the nylon to a 10ft length of willow, immediately ready with hook, line, sinker, and rod. The worms we used as bait were easily found under nearby rotting debris.

Despite the simplicity and crudeness of our gear, we landed many fish and during our forays learned much about fish behaviour and the relative importance of angler approach and appropriate tackle. The approach and angler skill we found paramount to success and the gear, particularly in luring fish as far as the hook, was very much secondary in the circumstances.

While we poked around the willows of the Clutha, we observed many trout cruising in their stillwater home, sipping flies. It was at this time I became most interested in flyfishing and soon acquired a cheap rod and flyline. The line was a gift from my uncle, one he'd used as a youth. It was a thin, level line with little weight, one that "took much driving", but nonetheless caught many trout.

As a stalking flyfisherman on the rivers of the South Island today, if I were still equipped with the same cheap, hollow glass rod, the tiny reel, and level line, I would still catch most of the fish I presently lure.

Five elements of gear represent essentials for flyfishing — rod, reel, line, leader, and fly. Of these, the leader and fly are the simplest and cheapest, but ones that require the greatest care in selection, preparation, and consideration of quality.

Flyrods have changed much during the last few decades, from natural materials such as cane, steel, fibreglass, and more recently, carbon, boron, and unclassified space age materials. With these improvements has come an undoubted improvement in quality, in the ability of rods to perform the function for which they are designed — propelling line a considerable distance.

Available to anglers is a very wide range of rods with an equal range of price. I own three. One is expensive, one a 7ft 6in lightweight used for small streams, a third a four piece for backpacking or fighting along bush tracks on a trail bike. However, while I enjoy using the most expensive rod, and marvel at the lightness and feel of the shortest, each allows me the same advantage in catching fish. Equally, the $45 Kilwell Midge I used for years would still be most satisfactory and do the same job. Ultimately, rods don't catch fish.

The vast majority of trout anglers seek — stalking anglers

particularly — feed within 60ft, with most approachable from 30ft to 50ft. These are not vast distances and any angler with reasonable skill should be able to cast a fly equally well with a host of different rods. The essential ingredient is the skill, not the equipment.

A fly reel is just a line holder. Its function is to house the line and allow it to be released during casting and again, with ease, when a fish is hooked and runs desperately away. Finally, the reel must have the capacity to collect line in the retrieve. Sophisticated drag controls, quick releasers, and other gadgets are quite unnecessary. What is necessary is simple maintenance on the part of the angler in ensuring free running, and then the hand skill and control during casting and playing fish.

While manufacturers have been developing an increasing sophistication and variety of rods and reels, they also have added imagination to new lines. Anglers can select from double tapers, weight forward, fast sink, and so on. Along with design variations come multitudes of colours, weights, and prices.

As a stream and lake edge fisher, I use just one line — a simple tapered floater purchased at a most moderate price. Having several reels, each with a different line, would add weight to my pack, but not improve my catch rate greatly.

Leaders can be purchased ready to use or constructed by an angler. I usually buy a manufactured one and add to the length with the best tippet nylon.

Leaders are a simple and cheap part of an angler's gear, but a part that should be considered and prepared most carefully, particularly for an angler stalking trout in clear waters.

What are the most important factors to consider about leaders? First, leader length. The function of the leader is to provide an invisible connection between fly and casting line. Logically, the longer this connection, the lesser the chance of a trout being alarmed by a visible line. I usually fish with a 16ft to 17ft leader, but do spend much time varying this according to conditions.

In a tailwind, I may lengthen or shorten it to make it easier to cast when a wind blows downstream. In tight fishing conditions, along a small stream or confined stream margin, again the leader may be shortened and then extended when very clear summer flows are encountered. The leader length is so important to success it may be necessary to vary it from one fish to the next as conditions or environment changes.

The second important consideration when preparing leaders is the nylon being used, especially at the tippet end. The two ideals aimed for are a line that is very fine, and one that is strong, primarily at knots.

The way a fly is presented may well be more important than the actual fly used. However, in terms of equipment, fly selection stands above the more expensive rod, reel, and line. Pattern, size, and style — nymph, wet, dry — are elements to consider. The selection should relate largely to the food the angler perceives trout are consuming.

The importance of the fly is confirmed by the number of books written on this subject and I'm not going to offer much here beyond highlighting the significance on which fly selection may be based.

In selecting a fly consider:

1] What time of year is it? Where I fish, I generally use weighted nymphs in the spring; consider beetles and then cicadas as the summer warms, and then mayflies through the later summer and autumn. As spring passes and summer arrives, the size of the nymphs generally diminishes. Along the willow infested streams in summer, a willow grub imitation is an intelligent choice, while on warm summer evenings a caddis may be more effective than a mayfly. The seasonal considerations are endless.

2] What is the depth of water being fished? And at what depth are fish feeding?

3] Are the fish taking nymphs or surface insects?

4]   What are the features of the insects being taken — size, colour, etc?

5]   What do I fancy using? For an experienced angler, an intuitive choice is often successful and is certainly one used with confidence.

In preparing to fish then, it has been suggested that the simplest elements of equipment are the ones deserving the greatest immediate attention, care, and angler skill. Flyfishing is, after all, a sport demanding a very high degree of skill.

In many sports a less skilled participant can out-perform a better player if equipped with superior gear. But in most forms of flyfishing an experienced angler with simple gear will be more successful than a less able angler equipped with the very best. The experienced fisherman, too, will take much time in preparing the leader and considerable care in selecting a fly.

Correcting The Casual Cast

BY MARK SHERBURN

We all make 'em. Botched casts that is. They can occur when it matters little, when you are alone casting to barren water. They will happen when we have an audience, or attempt instruction of a fellow angler and so cause embarrassment. They often take place during times of pressure or stress when fish catching opportunities are real. And they always occur when we lack concentration, doze-off into the relaxed, active slumber to which only a flyfisher can fully relate! These are flyfishing's "casual casts" and, while they are far from a criminal activity, believe me their correction will result in more enjoyable angling.

So, like me, if you've ever snapped your leader on a big trout where a wind knot once lived, slammed your dry fly down so hard it created bow waves big enough to surf on, or missed the trout of a lifetime by simply casting badly, then read on and discover some of the most frequently made casting mistakes, their usual causes, and some simple remedies.

Long days on the water can really take their toll. Sure, you're not likely to need a massage and pasta meal after every outing, but physical and mental fatigue, no matter how slight, will affect your performance with the rod. Ultimately, just like the athlete, training is the answer. Now before you start to panic, don't! I'm not for one moment suggesting gym work. But know that seasoned anglers, guides for example, fish all day, every day without casting problems or excessive fatigue. As such, the rest of us should either fish more or, more likely, take it easy!

Realistic casting distance and effort means attacking your day on the water at a rate that you can endure throughout the day and not blow fish catching chances at the end when your casting quality suffers.

Of course, just getting through the day can be an issue sometimes. I recall a day on the Tongariro some years back. It was to be my only day on the river that winter, so I really wanted to make the most of it. As luck would have it, the fishing was hot so I simply couldn't bring myself to stop fishing, not for lunch, not even for the call of nature. By three o'clock, with a couple of hours daylight left, my wrist and hand were aching with pain and I had to finally put the rod down and watch my mates catch some of the best fish of the day as a solid fresh run came through. On the way back home to Rotorua that evening, my wrist pain prompted a full investigation, so I did the math.

Let's say I made a modest five false casts per minute, times 60 minutes. That equals 300 false casts per hour, times say eight hours. Even taking fish playing time into account, that's well over 2000 false casts in a session!

Staggering how they add up, eh? Casting for a whole day (or whole week if you are lucky enough) is about pacing your effort to suit your ability. And both cast length and frequency can be factors.

Excessive, unnecessary false casting is common due to poor understanding, technique, or tackle. I've seen anglers inching line out cast after cast, making as many as 14 false casts per presentation! More false casts equal greater fatigue, increased chances of tangling, spooking, or wearing out your tackle. Actually reducing the number of false casts you make is easy. Remember the purpose of false casting (other than drying your fly) is returning the fly back to the action after line retrieval. Initially, pick up as much line as the situation makes practical. Obviously if you are fishing dries to super spooky fish, then ripping great volumes of line through the surface tension would be foolish, but equally don't retrieve the leader all the way back to your tip if you don't have

*Sight fishing
the Wilkin*
[PHOTO: DAVID
HALLETT]

*Wilderness
West Coast*
[PHOTO:
RAY GRUBB]

17

An angler dwarfed by Fiordland's beauty [PHOTO: DAVID HALLETT]

The angle of the cast is important to drag-free drift [PHOTO: DAVID HALLETT]

to. The backcast is exactly the same as the forward cast; you can shoot line, or deliver the fly with it. Shooting, or just slipping a little extra line into your backcast, makes sense if you are in a hurry, say for fast moving smelting trout, and it can eliminate one complete false cast, which based on the above calculations can save you 500 casts a day! Finally, the weight forward (WF) taper line is effectively a shooting head, with running line pre-attached. As such, it's designed to be shot once the head is clear of the tip. False casting your way through the running line simply wears you out and keeps the flyline companies in business as you wear it out! Modern good quality WF tapers also have slick finishes, which enables them to be shot much further than many anglers appreciate.

Now for wind knots. To the flyfisher, there is simply nothing much worse than the sudden slackening of line tension and straightening of a bent rod that can only mean a lost fish. Visual reassurance that the leader has parted at a wind knot can be enough to send even the most sainted in search of strong liquor. When the fly simply pulls free, you can concoct any excuse you care to dream up, but in the case of a wind knot there's no one to blame but yourself. Damn!

Tests prove that a simple overhand knot can reduce the tensile strength of your tippet by more than 50% — frightening if you started with just 1kg or 2kg. Although troubled with them, I've had a morbid fascination with wind knots since I began flyfishing. Just how they form so neatly in what must be a fraction of a second baffles me. Hell, I've even had wind knots in the flyline, so trust my advice here, I'm fully qualified!

Despite the name, wind knots are not caused by wind. It's true, windy conditions, particularly a head wind, will contribute to their frequency. But the simple, single most common reason is what's called a "tailing loop". This is where the upper most portion of the forward rolling loop kicks down below the lower portion, wraps, and tangles. Sound familiar? Frustratingly, it usually occurs on the final cast, just as you are about to present the fly and there's a good reason it does too. There's a natural tendency to "give it some oomph" on the final cast in order to achieve good distance, or punch the line into the wind. This excessive and sudden power as you begin the forward cast kicks the rod tip down and then rapidly back up. From that point onward, the dreaded tailing loop and its result, the wind knot, are inevitable.

Fortunately, this most common of casting problems is easily fixed. Don't change your casting power or timing as you begin the final presentation cast, but rather continue as you did when false casting, remembering to increase the power of the cast gradually until finally snapping the power into the end of the stroke and stopping the rod abruptly. I'm constantly amazed how a well timed, relaxed cast will go as far, sometimes further, than a poorly timed, overpowered one. If all else fails, make a habit of checking your leader at regular intervals, particularly at night or into a stiff breeze when your timing will be at its worst.

Finally, if you are at your wits end with tailing loop problems, consider a rod that has a smooth medium action — that is one that flexes evenly through most of the length of the blank.

Rod designs that have very soft tip sections and high stiffness butts are superbly useful fishing tools in the right hands, but need an even more delicate application of power in the forward stroke.

Tilt angle is another familiar casting problem. One of the things I like most about summer cicada hatches is slamming the fly down hard, catching fish, and making out I was trying to cast that way! Seriously though, without concentration delicate fly delivery can be a real effort. Equally, the opposite to our handy "slam-dunk-delivery" is where the line ascends going forward, runs out of power, and puckers in a trout-spooking series of curly twists. That one sounds familiar too?

Both problems can be reduced by looking at the angle of your casts relative to the water (I refer to this as the tilt angle) and the amount of energy in the cast as it turns over your fly.

Firstly, to make a good cast the forward cast and backcast should be aligned in a straight line — that is 180 degrees opposite to one another. So if you angle the forward cast down, say, 10 degrees, the backcast will need to be angled up by the same amount to maintain a straight line. So far no problem. In fact, this would normally make a good straight-line delivery. The difficulties of heavy delivery occur when the line is pointed down too severely, like in a head wind situation, or where the backcast needs to be pointed very high in order to clear some obstacle. In this situation, gravity aids the cast, so less energy is used, the line travels quicker, and turns over with a surplus energy, resulting in a fish-spooking splash! In the case of a high backcast, it can be difficult to slow down the line's forward momentum — one way is to open the loop to create drag. Do this simply by pushing the rod tip forward and down in more of an arc than normal.

Generally though, try to apply just enough power to turn over the fly, but no more. Any surplus energy as the loop uncurls will simply result in a splashy presentation. Excessive energy is fine when the cast is aimed high and you are going long. But short casts need an appropriate amount of energy and trajectory.

Sending the forward cast into a climb is a major cause of puckered, curly leaders on delivery. A good rule of thumb is to aim the forward cast downwards slightly towards an imaginary point just above the water's surface. The exception is when casting very long with the wind at your back. In this instance, use the wind to aid your cast by aiming high.

Slapping the water on the backcast can be the ruination of what happens out front. The result of lost forward momentum produces heinous tangles and, like the tailing loop, this annoyance usually occurs just as you are about to deliver that killer cast. Fishing the Rotorua lakes, deep wading at night, I often use this unique technique to test my blood pressure! A tired arm, low or no visibility on the backcast, an extreme backward tilt angle, and bringing the rod too far back in an arc are all causes. Most commonly, though, too little backcast power results in a lazy loop, which in turn succumbs to the relentless forces of gravity. Make sure you apply as much power to the backcast as you do the forward one. Force the tilt angle up a few degrees at the back and stop the rod abruptly at the end of the backcast to send the line rolling high and clear of the water. An easy fix, no matter what the cause, is simply to open your shoulders and watch most every cast until it has become almost second nature and you do it without thinking. After all, if you can't see the problem, you are unlikely to be able to correct it!

5 Point Casting Checklist

1]   Cast efficiently at a rate you can endure right through your day to avoid fatigue, aches, strains, and casting blunders.

2]   Shoot line quickly. Remember, false casting is about getting your fly back into a fish-catching location.

3]   For good presentations time after time, tilt the forward cast downward slightly at an imaginary point above the water. A high, climbing backcast will keep you from slapping the water behind you.

4]   Watch your backcast. If you can't see a problem, you'll have no chance of fixing it.

5]   Use the same technique in your presentation casts as you do in your false casts. Changing your timing or technique on the last cast will cause errors.

Get The Drift

BY JACK MACKENZIE

"The relative position of the rod tip and the fly is immaterial to the drift." This is a statement I often make while guiding anglers unfamiliar with maintaining long drag-free drifts — a statement often met with a curious look from the angler and one that deserves some explanation.

In many ways, the statement sums up two decades of personal experience flyfishing the rivers of New Zealand's south central North Island. Because trout in ultra clear New Zealand rivers often lie deep and sight their food at an incredible distance, long drift nymphing is a game that must be played, and played well, to successfully flyfish rivers such as the Rangitikei and Tongariro. Long drift nymphing is an interesting and demanding game with distinct rules.

A maximal degree of control over the drift can be achieved by using a floating line and a sinking pattern. Flyline behaviour is one of the important factors to understand. While on the water's surface, the flyline has a friction factor, which can make it behave like it is against a solid obstacle. When pushed or pulled sideways, the result can be as if the line were pulled around an imaginary post. By virtue of physical/mechanical advantage, drag can occur with alarming intensity.

The simplest example of this concept happens right at the rod tip. As the current moves by, the line at the rod tip tries to progress downstream. If the line is not retrieved, and/or the rod tip is not moved downstream correctly, a little "loop" or "belly" takes shape, just down current from the rod tip. The key factor here is the location at which the flyline leaves the water. It is the relative alignment of the rod tip and where the flyline leaves the water that can make or break the drag-free drift. Anglers often instinctively point the rod tip at the fly and ignore a malalignment causing drag at their feet.

Consider that physics dictates for every one metre that this "belly" moves down current away from the rod tip, the fly, at the far end of the flyline, must move down current two metres. This results in a 2:1 compound penalty in drag, behaving like a system of rope and pulleys.

But it is not just at the rod tip that drag can occur. A relaxed drift occurs when the far end of the flyline, leader and fly (terminal tackle) are all drifting along with the current, not being affected by a drift problem somewhere between the rod tip and the terminal tackle. At times, this is asking a lot and there are a lot of alligators in the swamp.

If rivers flowed along smoothly, the long drift nymphing task would be far easier. But then that would not be much fun would it? A further understanding of how to play the long drift game comes from understanding how river current behaves.

Rivers flow in three-dimensional ways. The horizontal components of flow are most apparent and are visible as surface movement. The vertical component of flow is perhaps the most subtle to understand. This vertical component, however, is responsible for a lot of the surface current movement.

When you observe the surface of a river, you'll see smooth areas, or slicks. Over-simplified, the smooth areas (slicks or boils) represent rising water. This can be caused by a subsurface obstacle, or by an over concentration of water underneath, resulting in an upwelling. When this rising water reaches the surface, it tends to spread out in all directions. Look at it like this: a river is like a conveyor belt moving along in a downstream direction. But on the surface of that conveyor belt, many "micro" events are occurring, in which the current is moving at different speeds and in different directions than the overall conveyor belt.

These events can contort a flyline and cause the same "mechanical advantage" drag as can occur at the rod tip. If for example, you place your flyline and a boil or slick occurs on one or both sides of the line, the result can be an "S" curve in the line, with each bend of the "S" carrying a 2:1 drag factor. It does not take Albert Einstein to see that this can be disastrous for the drift.

Another aspect of current that can be problematic is inconsistent current speed. Sometimes current at the bank can be non-existent, or even moving upstream in a back eddy, when the presentation zone beyond is moving quite fast downstream. This "differential" in current speed can cause a "macro" version of exactly the same phenomenon that occurs at the rod tip when the malalignment occurs with the flyline and rod tip. Generally, the greater the differential in current speed across which you lay the flyline, the more pronounced your drift problem will be and the quicker it will develop. This "macro" version problem can be harder to correct than the one at the rod tip, due to its potential magnitude and distance from the angler.

Various techniques exist for addressing drag. The most effective is avoidance. If you can spot one or more factors in the current that might cause drag, choosing the best angle of attack may alleviate, or even eliminate current-induced line deflections. For example, you spot a trout nymphing in relatively deep fast water about four metres from the bank. The water near the bank is a still zone. Rather than try to fish across that still zone, where drag will set in quickly, you choose to go way downstream so that you can place the bulk of the flyline in water that is moving in the same direction and at a similar speed as the fly. It may seem curious, but sometimes a 25 metre cast is required to approach a trout that is only four metres from the bank!

Another way to avoid drag in fast water with variable current is the high stick technique. By holding the rod tip high during the drift, the flyline can be kept above adverse currents occurring close to the angler.

When avoidance is not practical, another drift management

tool is the "mend". Mending is a very misunderstood tool and, improperly used, it can cause more trouble than it eliminates. A mend is a move by which a portion of the flyline near the angler is taken off the water and replaced in a more beneficial location to avoid drag-causing distortions on the flyline.

A couple of aspects of mending need mention here. First, attempting to mend a problem more than about 10 metres from the angler is almost always counterproductive to the drift. The amount of force needed to lift and replace line at distance will most likely pull or jerk the fly and terminal tackle. In its simplest form, a close proximity mend to maintain a relaxed alignment between the rod tip and the line can be very beneficial to the drift.

Another aspect of the long drift game is what I call the "window of drift". Simply stated, any cast has a resultant drift that is drag-free for a time. But, every drift will begin to drag at some point. If you accept this, then focus on the trout's window of awareness. In a given situation, any trout will be keenly aware of things within a certain distance. View this like a "circle of awareness". (Major events, like an angler in a clown suit, will be noticed at greater distance, of course.) But while feeding, trout will instinctively concentrate on items in the drift at a certain distance, which allows them to feed most efficiently.

Viewed this way, it follows naturally that the trick is to set up and maintain our window of drag-free drift to coincide with the trout's window of awareness. Sounds simple, doesn't it? So is walking across the swamp, until the alligators show up...

A further factor to understand is how to sink a nymph. Three contributing elements come in to play here:

1]   The sheer weight of the pattern. Obviously, heavier patterns sink faster. But extremely heavy patterns tend to drift unnaturally and can cause wary trout to question things. Also, building weight into a nymph can cause it to become too large, or disproportionate, let alone hard to cast. "Truck and trailer" rigs can address this problem, by using a large heavy nymph to get down and a length of additional tippet and smaller pattern tied to the larger hook shank or eye. Split shot also works, but can be cumbersome.

2]   Leader construction is significant. Simply stated, heavier, thicker line is more resistant to sinking. It has a resistance to movement through the water. Probably the most efficient leader for long drift nymphing is a length of tippet tied to the flyline. Leader purpose is often misunderstood. Tapered leaders are known to help air resistant dry flies turn over. Once on the water though, the thicker line performs poorly in the drift, especially when the vertical component enters into the equation. Weighted nymphs have far less need to be pushed out during the cast, because they gather kinetic energy during the cast and tend to carry beyond the flyline without help from the leader. For both dry fly and nymph, once on the water, long tippets are beneficial for the drift.

3]   The length of time and distance of drag-free drift determines the depth of presentation. This is relative to the preceding two factors, of course. When drag occurs, the very first thing that happens is that the nymph and leader are dragged upward in the water column. Any amount of drag-free drift can be considered an investment worth protecting. A good deal of thought needs to go into line management, so as not to sacrifice this investment.

With these basics in mind, a discussion on drift strategies follows. Although it is impossible to describe exactly what to do in each situation, some general principles become apparent.

Slack is your friend. This might go against some teachings and too much slack can cause difficulty. The closer to the terminal tackle the slack is, the more benefit it has. If a drift problem occurs in the main body of the flyline during a long drift, and slack exists out near the fly, then this reservoir of line can buffer the potential effects of the drag problem on the fly.

Some concern about strike effectiveness deserves mention. With a lot of slack in the drift, direct contact with the trout during a "take" might not be possible. But, because of the way the flyline behaves on the water, any sudden sharp major movement of the rod will impart movement of the fly. With a lot of slack in the drift, this sharp movement of the rod and resultant movement of the flyline is normally enough to implant the hook point into the trout's mouth, but not enough to "drive it home". Therefore, what happens immediately after the strike becomes significant.

Many anglers release the flyline from their trigger finger during a strike. This is bad practice at all times and particularly while fishing with a slack line. Recovering the line with the trigger finger is difficult and necessary if/when the trout runs back toward the angler. Techniques for recovering slack under these circumstances include running backwards, grabbing the flyline with the lips for stripping. You've seen (done?) it.

In flyfishing, it matters not so much that you know what you're doing, but more that you look good. Running backwards in an attempt to regain control of line released by the trigger finger during a strike looks bad, especially when you fall over. People will point and laugh.

The solution is simple: keep the line under your trigger finger during a strike. Be ready to quickly strip line immediately after the strike in order to make full contact with the fish. Once initial full and solid contact is made, it is a simple and easy matter to release line from the trigger finger, should the trout take off running.

Why fish with all the slack? Drift is king. In many places we fish, trout are educated and water is clear. A dragging fly not only does not get a take, but also often ends the game with a spooked trout making for cover. Once you learn to manage a slack line strike, the benefits outweigh the rest.

Another consideration is when to mend. Generally, if possible, make all your mends before the fly reaches the trout's window of attention. Set up your drift early and then try not to disturb it.

A poorly timed or excessively forceful mend can have two penalties:

28

1]   If a trout is watching your pattern and it is pulled during the mend, you will not get a take or may spook the fish.

2]   You will sacrifice penetration of a nymph or beneficial slack. A nymph sinks in part as a factor of time/distance of drag-free drift.

Mending short-range problems, close to the angler can be beneficial. I like a mending technique that uses the distant part of the flyline as an anchor, off of which the near part of the flyline is carefully lifted and replaced with improved alignment. Recognise that attempts to mend drift problems that are too distant from the angler can be counterproductive in terms of mend-induced drag and reduction of beneficial slack.

To mend or follow, that is the question. At the rod tip, alignment between the flyline and rod can be retained by either mending or following with the rod. During the drift, when the fly is in the trout's window of attention, I like to retain alignment by following with the rod tip, rather than chance subtle mend-induced drag by making a mend during this critical time. The result of this practice is often that the rod tip is pointed way downstream, well away from where the fly is, just to squeeze out that extra second of drag-free drift while the fly is in the strike zone. The principles of slack line strike apply here, if a take occurs.

This discussion can go on and on, as the situation parameters are infinite. One further situation, where the foregoing principles apply, is presenting a nymph to trout feeding deep in boils. Typically, where larger rivers make a corner and are deflected off a cliff wall, the current is forced downward and then wells up away from the cliff wall. You'll often see large trout feeding deep in such boils, typically head-down tail-up. These are tough trout to access.

Quite often the spreading action of the boil results in a backwash heading upstream on the inside of the pool. The difficulty in presenting to these trout is in slowing the flyline down, so the fly can penetrate. Cast too far left and the line is swept downstream, dragging the fly away from the boil. Cast too far right and the line is pulled up into the backwash and the fly goes with it (or visa-versa). But there is an exact place where the water breaks neither down the pool, nor into the backwash. Find that place and lay your line on the "break point". With the right leader and weight of fly, you can slow the line enough by finding this break point and you will get some penetration. Be patient and know that current in rivers is not constant. Current dynamics are such that the same exact cast, placed identically from the same casting location, can result in dramatically different drifts. Nowhere is this more apparent that in trying to "split the boil". Numerous casts are often needed to strike the exact set of circumstances that will allow a penetrating drift. Interesting game, often worth the effort.

When a trout is obligingly feeding at the surface, holding shallow, and watching the surface film, the need for long drift is absent. An angler need only place the fly in the correct "lane" an appropriate distance ahead of the trout. In this case, what happens with the flyline during the drift matters little, because the "slack reservoir" within the leader itself is sufficient to provide adequate time/distance of drag-free drift. But when you need that long drag-free drift for your presentation, the principles put forth here will become a matter for prime consideration. May you use them well.

Capturing Trout In Fast Water

BY TONY ENTWISTLE

Verlyn Klinkenborg visited New Zealand to fish in 1988 and later wrote this telling passage in *Esquire* magazine: "In American angling the deception, making the sale, and suckering the trout, is nearly all. But in New Zealand it just opens negotiations. New Zealand trout must be captured, not played. On a North Island river called the Rangitaiki a rainbow hopped before me, behind me, and forged a very large hook into an arrow, the curve bent out of it. On the Buller, a brown trout turned out of the slack into a current and peeled my reel. I started to sidestep downstream and looked to Tony (Entwistle) for counsel, who shouted "RUN!".". Run, that is, over a field of stone medicine balls. With 130 yards of line and backing out, the fish disappeared. On the Maruia, near Murchison, I turned the rod the wrong way for an instant as I sprinted beneath a low branch. When I looked back at my trout, away over there, it seemed as if he had fallen from a cloud."

To be a successful angler in torrid waters like the Buller requires more than just good spotting technique, fly selection, and casting. Catching fish means developing a good method for landing them too. In fast water, the skills of an angler have only just begun to be tested once the fish is hooked.

Playing, or as my friend Verlyn put it, "capturing" trout in fast water is a proactive game. Visualising what might happen, and being able to think ahead, is the first key to learning how to successfully land trout out of fast water.

In the visualising phase, before even casting, assess what's about, noting snags, big rocks, undercut banks, and anything a canny resident trout will head for once hooked. Look at how the current flows because it will be needed to help land the fish. The trout will use it to break off if you are careless. Consider, too, where to land the trout because it may well be too late when your face is full of fighting fish. That "where" may end up being several hundred yards downstream. This simple routine puts you one step ahead in playing any fish.

Next, be set to take the fight to the fish. It is natural to be careful when attached to something you don't want to lose. But being tentative will cost more in lost fish than if you learn to fight them hard from the start.

Taking the fight to the fish involves keeping solid pressure on most of the time, using the full arch of the rod and avoiding any slack in the line. It also means being decisive. During the fight when things are going the way of the trout, be prepared to give a little, quickly. But also be ready for moments to turn the fight your way and take the initiative.

Trout fishing's most dramatic moment follows the hookup. It may be the high drama of an explosive, head-shaking leap, a sizzling run, or the tense drama of a solid hit as the hook is set, followed by an even more solid thump of a really heavy fish as it surges into the current. It's the panic phase when whatever happens the angler has least control and the fish the greatest opportunity for escape. The trout is generally in panic, having just had his feeding routine rudely interrupted. The angler must cope not only with a panicking fish, but invariably with slack line retrieved in the earlier drift. For a moment the angler will be mostly reactive, but slack line must come under control. Keep the rod tip high and don't be tempted to rush for the bank.

If the fish runs away, controlling the line is not difficult. It's simply a matter of letting the line slide out freely under the forefinger of the rod-holding hand. The absolute no-no at this stage is to try and slow the trout down. It will be a lesson hard learned. I've watched many anglers clamp their hand around the reel and try to hold trout back. Doesn't work.

Should the fish turn and run towards you, strip in line, again under the forefinger of the rod hand, as fast as necessary to maintain contact with the fish, keeping a high arch in the rod. Normally, a decent fish in heavy water can't be held simply by forefinger pressure clamping the line to the rod grip. If it wants to run, let it.

If the fish stops running and slack still hangs below the reel, this is your first chance to be positively proactive. Seize the moment and wind line back on the reel as quickly as possible. Getting line back is an important achievement as it now leaves you free to manage the rod with either hand and to move without risk of line getting tangled around your feet or bankside obstacles. From now on don't miss the opportunity to retrieve line, even if it's only inches at a time.

By this stage, the trout will be in the current. Once a trout gets out 20 yards or more of line in hard current, it is very difficult to hold it back. If it is running straight upstream or downstream, simply hauling back on the line isn't likely to stop it. In fact, the opposite is more likely... the harder you pull one way; the harder it will pull in the opposite direction.

If the fish is across the stream, your efforts to rein it in will be compounded by the drag of the current across your line. The actual effect of this drag will be significantly increased line tension, especially at the moment the fish turns upstream. This counts at the weakest point in your line — either that wind knot you were unaware of, or the knot that holds the hook.

I have one simple rule that works best in these situations. Get that rod tip up as high as it can go with as much upward pressure as is reasonable. This lifts the fish to the surface. In deeper holes, this isn't going to happen immediately and may take several attempts. But by getting the rod high, the maximum amount of line will be kept out of the water and the most direct pressure possible can be applied on the fish's head.

The force of the current now starts to work for you in that it will help force the fish up as it gets in underneath it.

This stage of the fight isn't all proactive. The fish may make several runs where you must instantly ease the pressure, avoiding dropping the rod tip towards the trout with any significant tension — a common cause of breakoffs. This is also the time it may well choose to leave the pool. You either stand and watch, or go after it.

Now we come to the control phase, a time for manoeuvring the fish to your advantage, even as it's taking off down the rapids. If you've reached this stage, which may still be only a matter of seconds into the fight, chances are the fish is pretty well hooked. Now's the time to get to the bank, if it's feasible. I like to fight my fish from a position opposite and about a rod length below the fish so that the fish is just on my upstream side.

Every time the fish gets below, I attempt to gain control of its head by lifting with a rod angled slightly towards my bank until the fish stops moving. I'll now ease the pressure slightly and move around and down in an arc to take up the position described above.

As you follow a fish downstream, don't make the mistake of simply moving parallel to it, or in towards it. The pressure of the current is normally such that the fish simply translates the same distance and angle downstream as you move and you achieve nothing constructive towards landing it. The most often observed conclusion to this behaviour is to watch the angler walk the trout down to the tail of the pool where the sudden increase in tow of the current simply sucks the trout downstream into the rapids.

Because you are working on a tight line, use the tension to temporarily stop or "fix" the fish in position and work around it in an arc. The arc will be flattened or extended depending on whether you wind in line or the trout is able to gain line.

If a fish heads down the rapids, follow it, bearing in mind that the fish has to run out all your line and backing before things really get desperate. Again, keep the rod high, but always slanted towards the bank. The end result will see the current push the trout towards the bank where it can be directed into an eddy or

Tight line on the Ngaruroro River [PHOTO: DAVID HALLETT]

Stalking a West Coast spring creek [PHOTO: DAVID HALLETT]

Bliss on the upper Wanganui [PHOTO: DAVID HALLETT]

Small stream fishing is intimate and isolated [PHOTO: DAVID HALLETT]

Getting down and dirty on a South Island gem [PHOTO: DAVID HALLETT]

A typical stonefly imitation [PHOTO: BOB SOUTH]

Fiordland teems with fishable water [PHOTO: DAVID HALLETT]

Trout tucker on a stick [PHOTO: BLAKE MCDAVITT]

calm spot. Once the fish is at the bank, "fix" it by keeping the line tight and moving around it in an arc.

The ability to "fix" a fish while playing it is a learned touch — a combination of applied pressure from the angler balanced against the tension of the current. Too much applied pressure and the fish panics, struggling to pull away. Too little pressure and the fish is free to be swept away by the current. It is a very temporary state in the playing of a trout, often lasting only a few seconds. But "fixing" a fish is a valuable touch worth refining.

Once the trout is directly out from you, it is much easier to control its runs and apply even more direct pressure on its head. As soon as it hits the surface, "fix" it and attempt to apply lateral pressure to move the fish to you.

This lateral pressure is called sidestrain and is most effective when the trout is on the surface or within 10 yards of the angler. The mistake anglers most often make, myself included, is to apply sidestrain too soon, before the trout is actually in a suitable position.

For instance, if a trout is fighting even a yard below the surface and is still in heavy current, the cross current drag as you lower the line into the water is substantial. To a point, this may actually help turn the fish's head, but on fine tippets and small hooks the margin for error is small.

The closer a trout comes to an angler, the lower the rod tip can be dropped to the side (not forward) and the more direct the sidestrain can be applied to its head. Inside the last few yards, the rod tip may be almost at water level. During the latter part of this control phase the angler will be mostly proactive.

Often big browns in shallow water save the best of their fight for last. This is now the landing phase. When a brown comes into the shallows don't simply assume the fight is finished. Watch its head. As it turns out, expect another run. As it straightens upstream or downstream, apply sidestrain and draw the trout back in.

Apart from the first few seconds in panic phase, this landing phase is when most fish are lost, as anglers lock on the fish trying to rush it to the net. It is tempting to rush, but this phase, particularly with browns, may take the longest to complete. It is a phase of give and take with the trout making repeated, but decreasingly powerful runs. Some anglers are prone to play the fish to a standstill here. That's not the idea either. The principle of taking the fight to the fish still applies and anglers should make a conscious effort to end the fight as expeditiously as possible so the fish can be released in a fit state or dispatched humanely.

This is the time of capture — a moment where I prefer to use a net to lessen physical damage to the fish and facilitate handling for release.

In the latter stages of playing the fish, use mostly a low, side-angled rod. At the point of netting, raise the rod high again with full upward pressure and attempt to get the fish sliding across the surface. It's always a prudent precaution to get someone to help net a very large fish.

These then are the basic principles of fighting fish in fast water:

o   visualise the action and think ahead

o   put pressure on fish at a distance, use a high rod to clear line from the water, apply upward pressure

o   make the current work for you by keeping the rod angled slightly towards the near bank

o   learn to "fix" a fish in position so you can move around it

o   play fish from a position opposite and slightly below it

o   be prepared to follow the fish

o   apply maximum sidestrain as the fish gets closer

- at all times be prepared to instantly relieve the pressure on the fish and let it run if it wants

- lift the fish's head at the moment of netting

Finally, at any time during a fight, when you need to think or look around, stick the rod above your head. Also, if the fish is fighting too hard and direct pressure doesn't help, try taking off the pressure. You might be as surprised as the trout when it stops dead in its tracks. But be ready — the trout won't stop for long. The next move is yours.

Getting Down And Playing Dirty

BY DAVID MOATE

Nymph fishing is arguably the most effective flyfishing method today because in the majority of waters a trout's diet is mainly invertebrates.

Nymph fishing is the backbone of flyfishing in New Zealand and the basic skills must be mastered to provide consistent success. Anglers who improve these basics and become very good nymph anglers frequently enjoy successful fishing throughout the year on all types of waters.

While any flyfishing outfit can be used for nymph fishing, the right tackle always gives an advantage. A 9ft to 9ft 6in fast action, powerful rod from #5 to #7 will cover most of the country, with #8 and #9 rods ideal for the Tongariro and other large rivers. Match this with a high quality weight forward floating line, with a heavy taper designed for casting weight. Also ideal is a line one size heavier than the rod, which loads the rod quickly for short to medium casts, but does not overload for long casts. A dark coloured line will not disturb trout as much as a light one, but can be difficult to see. Try olive green as a compromise, or only darken the first five metres.

Nymph fishing requires a lot of casting, so keep the line clean, stretched, and apply plenty of line shooting chemicals and floatant paste. Carry a variety of nylons to cover a range of situations — stiff nylons for wind, heavy flies and leader butt sections, soft nylons for delicate presentations, and stillwater and fluorocarbon nylons for when shadow is a problem. A range of indicators and quality floatant paste is important.

The first key to being a good nymph angler is to plan how to fish a section of water before starting. Part of that planning involves getting in a position to be able to most efficiently and effectively fish the water. Factor in casting obstructions, trout wariness, and safety. But most importantly, selection of a casting position is about being able to cast onto the water to give the best drift, placing the nymph exactly where intended with the minimum of effort. Remember, every inch of that flyline in the water affects the drift and a casting position that reduces line drag, mending requirements, and the number of casts required greatly increases success. If you want to see just how important positioning is, watch a busy pool on the Tongariro and take note of where the successful anglers are in relation to the lies they are fishing. Positioning is equally important in stillwater, whether fishing from the shore or boat. Rather than simply trying to cover the water, position yourself to bring the nymph along gaps in the weed, dropoffs or ledges, where trout leave the security of cover to hunt nymphs.

If numbers of trout are the order of the day, grid the section of water to be fished. Start at the furthest downstream fishy area and move upstream systematically, covering all likely areas, from shallow to deep, and close to further away. Take all hooked trout downstream away from undisturbed water.

Change tippet length and fly weights and patterns to suit the different types of water rather than be lazy and persist with the one rig. Areas that are difficult to get a good drift into should be tried from different positions until you get the best drift; these are the areas you frequently get better fish because other anglers have not fished it well. If it is larger fish you are after, first locate all the areas with good bed structure, cover, water depth with the best feeding options, as this is where the larger fish will be. Plan to fish each area from the best location to put the nymph through at the right depth and speed to tempt that big trout. A nymph that is tumbling along the streambed will be taken confidently, or if ignored will not disturb wary trout. Poorly placed and presented nymphs dragging through a trout lie will usually scare fish, or result in missed strikes. Planning the best way to fish a section of water will, with practice, take only a few minutes and will offer more rewards than simply fishing the best and most obvious water first.

Once a decision is made on how to fish a section of water, the next step is to select nymph patterns that will catch trout. A good formula to aid nymph pattern selection is to prioritise the attributes the pattern must have to catch trout in a particular location.

First step is to get to the trout, second to catch its attention, and third to fool it into eating the fly. Step one in the selection process is to determine the pattern's weight and size.

Step two should determine whether it will be an attractor or imitation pattern. Step three is to decide on the pattern's general appearance and any special features it may have — for example, movement, trapped air bubbles, or slim profile. Practising this formula will enforce why particular patterns work well in some situations and not others. It will foster pattern development or help an angler make wise purchases and, in time, it will create a flybox full of nymph patterns that can be fished with confidence.

The next step is to select the best rig to fish the chosen water effectively and efficiently and, of course, always trying to match the rig with the nymph patterns to be used. Do not be lazy by persevering with a rig that is simply unsuitable for the occasion. Attention to detail here makes a huge difference to success. Prioritise the rig to be used in the following order.

Step one: construct the leader to cast well in the given conditions and for the pattern selected. This is the first priority simply because, if an angler cannot cast efficiently and accurately, trout will not be caught. The only compromise in this step is casting ability. For example, in a clear deep pool a 5m leader is required to not disturb wary trout. But if accurate casts of only 3m are capable of being made, the angler should split the difference, so there's still a chance of casting well, rather than leaving the pool frustrated and the trout wiser.

Step two: choose the right indicator and set it up properly so it sets the depths of the nymphs, detects strikes, and informs of drag. For long deep drifts or in fast water, a bigger indicator is required. In shallow stillwaters, or when stalking for wary trout, a small obscure indicator will do the job, or even no indicator.

Step three: set up the whole rig to work as efficiently as possible, which may require greasing the leader butt section to aid mending, adding split shot, double rigging, or selecting different types of nylons for the tippet.

Again, practising these steps will help anglers understand why a particular rig works well and which rigs are the most efficient to use. While initially this will take up valuable fishing time, it will pay dividends ten fold. Those nymph anglers who do not bother being so meticulous and experimental will become more frustrated and waste a lot of time. For deep water nymphing, use heavier rods to facilitate casting longer distances, or handling double rigs. The angler should take a position beside or above the fishy area and cast upstream enough to allow the nymphs to sink to the bottom.

Plan the presentation so all mends are complete and full control is achieved by the time the nymph is moving through the fishy area.

The indicator should twitch as the nymphs tick the riverbed, indicating that they are in the strike zone. If this doesn't occur, keep trying until it happens. Getting the right depth may require experimenting with pattern weight and tippet length, or adding split shot. Fish each drift as far downstream as possible to maximise chances and then swing the nymph, twitch in several metres, and recast. Double rigs are very productive in deep water, as they fish several depths and in clear waters they do not spook wary fish as much as large patterns. Deep pools are prime trout habitat, but these can be very difficult to fish due to variable currents and upwelling. The trick with trout tantalisingly gliding in an upwelling is to carefully study the water flow to locate the line of current that will take the nymph deep, rather than push it to the surface. This current is usually right on the line between the upwelling or back swirl and the main flow, and requires plenty of weight and mending to get the nymphs to the trout. In extreme situations, use a long thin leader, no indicator, and feel for the strike. Foam lines, or patches of foam trapped in back eddies, are great areas to drift or hang a deep nymph, especially along the far bank because trout love to hide under the rocky ledges and slip out for a drifting snack. In stillwaters, finding the depth at which trout are feeding is the secret. Clear intermediate sinking lines with unweighted patterns, or a floating line and very long leader with weighted patterns, are the two choices of tackle. Select areas trout will hunt nymphs and try different depths and retrieve speeds until the action is uncovered. In windy conditions, a large indicator can be used to suspend the nymphs and bob them around — easy fishing, but fun and effective.

When stillwater nymphing, it pays to try double rig nymphs, placed 1m apart. Slowly troll these from a float tube, rowboat, or canoe. Pause between movements and stop occasionally to fish a variety of depths and speeds. On windy days, lines of white foam, called wind lanes, will concentrate food and invariably represent an under-utilised angling opportunity. Drifting and working nymphs along these lanes can produce spectacular fishing. I have had great sport exploiting these wind lanes from the shoreline, or from a boat with a sea anchor deployed in lakes such as Kuratau near Taupo, Rerewhakaaitu near Rotorua, and Dunstan in Otago. Sinking lines and floating nymph patterns imitating snails and damselfly larva are deadly when used over weedbeds, dropoffs, and in channels.

When shallow water nymphing, use an indicator system that permits quick and frequent adjusting to set the nymphs at the correct depth. In shallow, fast water look for the hollows in the riverbed, or, if visibility is poor, watch for the flat smoothish patches that appear. Target these spots and use short accurate casts and short drifts to quickly check out each spot. Casting from the side will give the most controlled drift and help prevent the fast water sucking down the flyline. It also allows the angler to only put the nymph through the fishy area.

If forced to cast from behind the trout, hold the rod high and rod arm outstretched to keep as much flyline off the water surface as possible. For longer casts and drifts in fast, shallow water, keep plenty of slack upstream of the rod tip to prevent a loop dragging your line. One shallow area frequently missed by anglers on larger waters is the tailouts of pools and runs. These areas are usually rocky and shallow, but when water temperatures are 16–19°C trout can be found in surprising numbers in these locations. When stalking trout cruising shallow waters, either suspend the nymph above the weeds or bottom and in the path of the trout. As it approaches, pull in 30cm of line smoothly to lift the nymph without disturbing the water surface unduly. Time the lift so as not to disturb the approaching trout and so it will arrive in time to see the nymph dropping back down. The other option is to leave a nymph lying on the bottom and quickly twitch it off the bottom when the trout is about 1m away.

By mid-summer, low clear waters and fishing pressure make trout wary and easily disturbed. When nymphing for these wary trout, use presentations that keep as much of the leader and flyline out of the trout's sight to improve success. Stay to the side and cast well upstream, then drift only the tippet and nymphs into the trout's feeding zone. Use aerial mends, such as reach casts. And overpower or underpower the cast to flick the leader and fly downstream of the flyline to give drag-free drift and further keep the flyline away from the trout. When possible, use leaders up to 6m, with fine tippets and small, slim nymphs. To get depth, cast further upstream, heavily weight the fly, or use lead shot or putty. Keep indicators small and dull coloured. For super touchy trout, do not use an indicator. Instead, watch the trout open its mouth and take the nymph, or grease a 30cm section of leader to act as an indicator. Keeping a low profile and casting from an unorthodox location will help fool a few wary trout.

Many trout during a hatch only target the emerging nymph, instead of the hatched dun. A rise that frequently only exposes the trout's back or tail indicates this is what is happening. When nymphing during a hatch, use a dark coloured indicator or dun imitation and double rig, with a nymph pattern that copies the natural.

If possible, target individual trout and time the rises so you can drift a nymph past it shortly after a rise. Experiment with the depth of the nymph to ensure the nymph is drifting at the level the trout is holding.

Looking Downstream

BY PETER CHURCH

The big rainbow moved deep in the pool, there was a flash of white mouth followed by a shower of water, silver, and red as the fish jumped. A few minutes later the fish is in the net, admired, and released. A typical scene played out in the backcountry every summer except this fish was not taken by the standard New Zealand technique of upstream nymph fishing, but on a small traditional wet fly fished downstream on a sinking line.

Upstream nymph fishing is a highly successful technique on most New Zealand waters and dominates the way most Kiwi flyfishermen approach the water. Yet downstream wet fly, or streamer fishing can be very effective in many situations. Fishing downstream can also extend fishing opportunities at times when water, weather, or fish behaviour may not suit nymph fishing.

Wet fly and streamer methods of flyfishing involve swinging the fly across the river on a tight line, the opposite of upstream nymph and dry fly where the objective is to present the fly as a food item drifting naturally in the current. Upstream fishing usually involves having slack line on the water and, because of this, timing the strike is visual. Fishing downstream, the river current will keep some pressure on the line so the fisherman remains in contact with the fly all the time, feeling the bite. The current will also add action to the fly. This can be increased by manipulation of the rod and line by the fisherman.

Why does swinging the fly across current work? We will never know the correct answer, but fishing theory will always try to provide an answer. The fly may look like a piece of food, it may be invading personal space, or the fish is just curious. Take your pick.

In New Zealand, the definition of wet fly fishing has become muddled by the use of the term in the Taupo and Rotorua areas where wet fly fishing has always involved using sinking lines and streamers, or lure type flies.

Why go downstream? The feeding behaviour of trout often dictates the use of the wet fly or streamer. When fish are feeding on baitfish, smelt, whitebait, or bullies, fishing a streamer can be the answer. The problems of the evening rise can often be overcome by swinging a small wet fly in the surface. If the rise continues on well after dark, using the wet fly allows the fisherman to continue because the fly can be fished by feel.

The type of water is another good reason to look downstream. On large rivers, downstream fishing is often the only way to cover all the water. Big, wide, slow-moving pools can be fished very effectively by a streamer, particularly on some areas where it is not possible to drift a nymph. The wet fly can work in the fast current on the edge of backwaters. Fast water, particularly riffles, provides great areas to swing the fly downstream. The broken water surface helps hide the fisherman and the line falling on the water. Trout lying in fast water have little time to inspect a food item or a fly, meaning the take can be an instinctive grab, resulting in a very positive strike for the angler. An approach that works well on many streams is to fish upstream in the best places with nymph or dry fly, then turn around and fish back downstream.

Physical conditions can also determine when to use the downstream approach. On many rivers, cliffs, and bluffs can restrict access to good casting positions and often the only way to get a fly in front of a fish is from above. On windy days, fishing downstream is often the only way to get a fly on the water. In fact, it can become an ally. Get the wind on the opposite shoulder to the casting side and it is possible to throw the line across the river

— maybe not always in the right place, but the wind-ruffled water surface will help disguise the line fall.

Reaching the river and finding high or discoloured water is always a big negative. Fishing a streamer, particularly if the river is dropping after a flood, can be effective. There is a window of opportunity when the water is still coloured, but not too dirty, when the fish will often feed aggressively. Some fisherman will deliberately target these time periods knowing the coloured water will mean the fish are easier to approach and fool.

Looking straight into the sun makes seeing a strike indicator or dry fly impossible. Using downstream techniques, which rely on feeling the strike, can help overcome these difficult conditions.

Streamers, or lures as they are commonly called in New Zealand, are fished to imitate baitfish such as smelt, whitebait, bullies, even freshwater crayfish. Large trout will not pass up the opportunity to feed on these large mouthfuls. This is the reason most streamers are tied in large sizes. Traditional lures like the Rabbit, Matuku, and Fuzzy Wuzzy were all developed to imitate these foods.

Basic streamer fishing is very simple. The cast is made cross-stream, allowing the fly to swing back until the fly hangs below the angler. The rod follows the swinging fly so that the fisherman stays in contact with the fly. The tight line means the angler will feel the bite immediately the fish takes, and lifting the rod tip should result in hooking the fish. A straight line also means the strike does not have to be violent — too much power and the trout will break off.

Using a fixed length of line in this manner relies on the current to put action on the fly, which is fine in fast water. But in slower water, the angler needs to put action on the fly. Remember, the fly is imitating a live creature. There are several ways of adding life to the fly. Raising and lowering the rod tip as the fly swings will make the fly dart like a baitfish working across current.

Pulling or stripping the flyline with the line hand can make the fly work in a very life-like way. Experiment with different tactics and retrieves. Some days the trout will want the fly to be fished fast with erratic movements. On other days, slow and deep will work better.

Many experienced anglers will let the fly hang for a moment below them, then retrieve the fly a couple of pulls before lifting into the cast. This tactic allows for any trout that has followed the fly across the current to take on the hang. If they do not hit the fly at that moment, pulling it away from the fish will often encourage a strike. This is also a practical move because the line must be shortened before the next cast can be made.

The depth at which the fly is fished is also a variable in streamer fishing. There is a large range of sinking flylines on the market to help the angler get his fly down and, while some of the new sink-tip lines are ideal for streamer fishing, it is not necessary to rush out and buy one. It is possible to use a floating or slow sinking line if the local regulations allow the use of weighted flies or spilt shot on the line. To get deeper with these lines, use a longer leader and adjust the weight until the fly is getting down close to the bottom. On many of the larger rivers, there is no getting away from using a fast sinking line to get deep enough.

Mending the line as it swings across the current is critical for two reasons. First, mending the line slows the swing down and keeps the line reasonably straight on the water, so contact is kept with the fly. Second, an immediate mend will throw slack line, allowing the fly and line to sink before the line starts swinging across the current. It can be necessary to mend the line two or three times, depending on how the line reacts in the current, on each swing. If fast water causes a big downstream belly in the line, lift the rod tip and roll the line back upstream. If that belly is left on the water it will cause the fly to speed up unnaturally on the swing, lifting it off the bottom and defeating the purpose of getting it down deep in the first place. The same is true if an upstream belly forms on the water — a downstream mend is necessary. Mending the flyline is a skill that requires a little practice, but once mastered will improve the catch rate.

Fishing downstream allows the fisherman to cover a lot of water relatively quickly, but it is important to cover all the water. This is done by methodically working down the likely fish-holding areas, taking a step at a time, covering the water in a series of big arcs. If the water is slow or shallow, angle the cast more downstream so the fly does not sink as deep on the swing and snag on the river bottom. To get the fly fishing deeper, angle the cast more upstream, giving it more time to sink.

Time of the day has a part to play in streamer fishing. The low light opportunities early in the morning and in the evening, of course, are prime times. But a cloudy day can be productive as well. Night fishing has long been an accepted part of New Zealand trout fishing and it is almost exclusively streamer or lure fishing. It is without doubt a great time to catch large fish.

The standard #6 to #9 rod used by most trout fishermen will do the job. It must match to the right line weight too. A heavier rod can be an advantage at times when throwing big flies in the wind. The angler is faced with multiple choices of lines and it can be quite confusing. If using a floating line, stay with the standard floating line — that part is easy. Sinking lines need some explanation.

Most line manufacturers rate their lines by sink rates — Type 1 being the slowest, up to Type 6 the fastest. These lines can be full sinking lines or sink-tip, where only a length of line at the front will sink, and the rest will float. The front sinking section will also be rated on sink rate.

When purchasing a sinking line, take into account the type of water it will be fished in. The deeper the water, the faster type of sinking line needed. Many of these lines can also be very useful for lake fishing. The advantage of the sink-tip lines is they are easier to mend on the swing because of the float section. There are now some very specialised lines on the market for streamer fishing. They are sink-tip lines with a very fast sinking line section, usually five to 10 metres long. These lines were developed for use in big, fast water and are excellent on rivers like the lower Mohaka.

The decision to use weight forward lines or double taper lines is a personal one and involves a compromise. The weight forward line is easier to cast in theory, but can be harder to mend on the water because the thinner back section of line may not have enough weight to help with rolling the line over. The double taper line will overcome this problem, but is harder to distance cast.

There is a huge range of streamers and lures available in New Zealand today. One pattern that stands out for its all-round fish-catching ability is the Woolly Bugger. The reason for the success of this simple pattern is the amount of movement the fly has swimming in the water. The soft marabou tail flutters in the water in a very life-like way. This is enhanced by working the rod and flyline. If movement is one key to a successful streamer, the silhouette is the other key ingredient. The Muddler Minnow, with its large clipped deer hair head, provides a generic fish shape that imitates a number of different baitfish species.

The colour of the fly is always a great debate. Matching the colour of the fly to the colour of the food item being imitated is a good starting point. For example, the Grey Ghost is a great smelt imitation. However, many streamers look like nothing represented in nature, yet they will still catch fish. As a general rule, fish a dark fly in discoloured water and low light situations. The theory is that the dark fly will give a better silhouette, making it easier for the fish to see. In bright conditions use a light coloured fly.

Fly size is a consideration. Again, a general rule is the less visibility the larger the fly used. Following this rule, dirty water needs a large fly, a number two for example. Low clear water may require a much smaller pattern, #8 to #10.

Many of the flies are generic and have spawned many variations, like combining a Muddler with a Rabbit to produce a fly with bully shape and good movement in the tail. Some of these variations, available in tackle shops, include the Woolly Bugger, Rabbit series, Parsons' Glory, Muddler Minnow, Hamill's Killer, Doll Fly, and Red Setter.

A special leader is not needed. A level piece of nylon in the 2–4kg range will do the job. Normal leader length is around two to three metres. If going deep, shorten the leader to keep the fly swimming close to the riverbed.

Traditional wet fly fishing has been around for a long time. In fact, it is how flyfishing evolved. Wet fly fishing imitates a number of different insects that end up submerged in the river and their

Still morning bliss on a Rotorua lake [PHOTO: DAVID HALLETT]

Putting back a Waiau River rainbow on a drift fish trip
[PHOTO: DAVID HALLETT]

Polaroiding a tailout [PHOTO: DAVID HALLETT]

It's a wee jumper [PHOTO: DAVID HALLETT]

Crossing the Ngaruroro [PHOTO: DAVID HALLETT]

Presentation is paramount on the Mohaka catchment's Te Hoe River

[PHOTO: DAVID HALLETT]

No room for casual casting in wilderness rivers [PHOTO: DAVID HALLETT]

The Ngaruroro offers deep pools as well as fast water nymphing

[PHOTO: DAVID HALLETT]

behaviour; such as emerging mayfly and caddis nymphs; insects drowned during egg laying, or spent and sucked down by fast water. Even drowned, wind-blown terrestrials during summer, such as beetles, ants, spiders, bees and wasps, can play an important part in trout diet.

Many of the fishing techniques discussed in the section on streamer fishing also apply to the wet fly. The basic cast is made across stream, a mend is made if necessary to slow the swing of the fly, and the rod tip follows the fly. Imitating insects does not require as much action to be put on the fly as streamer fishing. Fast water and riffles will impart enough movement on the fly to make it attractive to the trout. In slower moving water, using a slow retrieve may be needed to put action on the fly. The trout will often take when the fly is hanging directly below the angler, so leave the fly on the hang for a moment in case a trout has followed the fly as it swims across the river. Even move it from side to side with the rod tip. Keep false casting down to a minimum. Trout are not flying fish. The more time the fly is in the water, the better. Also, casting the fly will dry it out, slowing the sink rate. It is important that the fly sinks as soon as it hits the water so that it swims in or just under the surface film. Start working with short casts and then lengthen to cover all the water. Do not wade unless necessary as it is easy to spook shallow-lying fish.

On New Zealand streams, most of the best wet fly opportunities occur when the trout are feeding on or near the surface. Insects get caught in the surface film and offer easy targets for feeding trout. The peak time for this is on the evening rise. If the trout ignore the fly on the floating line, you may need to sink the fly a little. Use a small split shot placed a few centimetres above the fly, or treat the leader so it will sink.

There are some commercial preparations available that will help make the leader cut through the surface tension. Otherwise, a simple riverbank solution is to take the shine off the leader by rubbing it with dirt or sand. The other option is to use a slow-sinking line that will put the fly just below the surface of the stream. The term wet fly action or dry fly action was often used to describe fly rods many years ago. This was for a practical reason: wet fly rods had a softer action in the tip to help absorb the shock of a fish taking the fly on a straight line. With no slack in the line as the fly is swinging, the pressure of the take goes directly on the rod tip. Most modern rods are made with fairly stiff tips. This presents a problem when an active feeding trout smashes at the fly tied on a light leader. Break-offs do happen! To overcome this problem, do not strike. Let trout hook themselves and keep the rod tip up in the air as the line swings. The belly created between the rod tip and the water surface will also help absorb some of the strike.

As the wet fly swings across the river, it reaches a point where a combination of current and pressure on the line will cause the fly to start lifting away from the riverbed. This rising action on the fly is the hot spot on the swing, as the fly must appear to be a hatching insect starting to rise to the surface.

As aquatic insects rise to the surface, they often have an air bubble surrounding their body. This is why many of the fly patterns have flashy materials in the dressing.

It is common in many countries to fish the wet fly in a team. Up to four or five flies can be used on one leader. Without doubt, this technique works very well in attracting trout to the fly. In New Zealand, most areas restrict the number of flies on the line to two. This is still a good idea. Try using different combinations. Two is enough. Imagine the tangles with five flies on the line.

As most of the flies used for wet fly fishing are small, #10 down to #18, a heavy rod is not necessary in most situations. A #5, #6, or #7 rod will do the job on most rivers and streams. Tapered leaders will help present the small flies better than a level one. A light tippet is also a requirement to help present the flies. Use 2–3kg. The thinner tippet allows the flies to swim in a more natural manner.

There are thousands of wet fly patterns and this can be daunting for a beginner. There are two basic groups: bright gaudy flies, which are more like lures, and the more natural, sombre looking flies. Many of the old patterns have a wing in the dressing. The modern trend is more towards a simple fly with just a hackle. Flies dressed this way are often called spiders. The hackle is the collar of feather wound at the head of the fly and it is the key to the success of many wet flies. Most are tied with soft feathers to provide plenty of life-like movement in the water. The most successful flies are tied slim. The beginner is best to select six to 10 patterns in different hook sizes from #10 down and stick with them. These might include the Red-tipped Governor, Red Tag, March Brown, Black Gnat, Greenwell's Glory, Red Spinner, Hughie's Bug Spider, Mylar Spider, Peacock Spider, and Mallard and Claret.

The Full Take On Dry Fly Fishing

BY DAVID MOATE

Catching a trout rising to the surface to take a dry fly is undoubtedly one of the great experiences flyfishing offers. So much so that it becomes instantly addictive. New Zealand dry fly addicts have many opportunities to satisfy their dry fly fishing dreams on a huge range of waters and situations and exploring ways to maximise dry fly fishing opportunities will only intensify the addiction.

An angler's favourite flyfishing rig will be suitable for dry fly fishing, but to match most New Zealand situations the ideal outfit is a 9ft to 9ft 6in fast action rod. Three to five weight rods are ideal for small streams, or where delicate presentation is required. Otherwise #6 or #7 rods will cover the country. For most dry fly fishing, a weight forward, floating flyline matched to the rod with a longish front taper is ideal.

Exceptions to this are when fishing larger patterns, or casting into strong winds when a line weight heavier than the rod, with a shorter taper, will cast easier. A dark coloured flyline does not spook trout as much as bright coloured lines and is a major advantage on clear waters. Leaders need to be constructed to suit the situation, with stiffer nylons for casting into the wind, for casting large patterns, or as a leader butt section to aid turnover and accuracy. Soft nylons are a must for stillwater or delicate presentations. Fluorocarbon tippets help in similar situations, especially stillwater dry fly fishing, or anywhere nylon shadow is a problem. A good quality fly floatant and a drying patch on the vest are important tools.

Learning to anticipate conditions that will encourage trout to take a dry fly is one of the keys to success. Casting a dry fly may be pleasant, but it soon loses appeal when nothing takes. Equally, not recognising dry fly fishing opportunities and missing out is frustrating. Weather, water temperatures, humidity, barometric pressure, and seasonal appearances of concentrated food are the key elements that influence trout to surface feed.

Weather plays a huge part, as it impacts on all the other conditions that influence surface feeding. Long term weather patterns dictate water temperature, flows, and insect lifecycles and densities. Short term weather conditions can create exciting dry flyfishing opportunities, such as when rain and wind flush many insects, like beetles or cicadas, into the water. The classic mayfly hatch is greatly affected by water temperatures and humidity, as they dictate whether a rise will happen or not. Water temperatures affect trout more than the insects hatching, with many an evening hatch happening with no fish rising due to high water temperatures. Temperatures from 13–18°C are ideal for trout activity throughout the day and night. Below this, surface activity is only likely to happen during the warmest part of the day. Above this, and anglers may have to target the cooler parts of the day. Hatching insects, especially caddis and mayflies, require calm and humid conditions to successfully hatch, fly to cover, and then return to breed. The influence of barometric pressure on trout activity, especially surface feeding, is interesting and variable. Generally, falling pressure is negative until humidity increases and the weather breaks. This often produces hatches that trout often respond to, or the weather change can wash lots of food into the water. I have experienced this many times; with poor fishing until the weather breaks and trout begin to feed actively. One afternoon in the Grey River, as the rain became very heavy, 26 large brown trout took one very battered and wet #10 Royal

Wulff. Rising pressure with clearing weather and waters provides the best conditions for surface feeding activity. Do not be afraid to dry fly fish discoloured waters, as trout will see the fly and are often in vulnerable locations and actively feeding.

Another key to dry fly fishing is pattern selection. Trout can become selective when surface feeding, only taking a particular type and size of insect. Trout feeding during a hatch, or when a certain insect is prolific, become quite fastidious and a good imitation is required to fool them. A pattern that is the right size, shape, and colour, and simulates the natural's movement, or how it floats, will be the most successful. Studying the trout rise form will also give vital clues in pattern selection. A full head rise indicates the natural is riding on the surface film, like a hatched mayfly dun expanding its new wings prior to flying away.

A splashy rise means a moving target, such as caddis or stoneflies that flutter across the water surface. A slurpy rise, which only leaves small rings, means trout are taking the duns that are trying to break through the surface film to hatch. A rise that bulges the surface and where the trout's tail breaks the surface means they are taking spent spinners dead or dying, lying flat on the surface, or beetles just below the surface. Large insects, such as cicadas, stoneflies, blowflies, and craneflies, usually prompt explosive rises.

Attractor patterns catch lots of trout and can be used in many situations. They will bring up trout from deeper water, or out of cover, better than natural imitations, so they are great for searching the water and exploring new areas. Attractor patterns used during a hatch can be very successful. Lee Wulff described this as "the strawberry in the cream" and attractors are really useful if the natural pattern cannot be worked out, or an angler has difficulty seeing it. Attractor patterns either resemble a range of terrestrial insects that represent a desirable meal for a hungry trout, or a range of natural imitations that can be used in most hatch situations. The "attractor" aspect of these patterns is something that stands out (to the trout) — movement, silhouette, or colour — which triggers their predator or familiarity response.

Double rigging is effective with dry flies in the right situation. During hatches, a combination of an attractor and natural will increase takes of the natural, with the odd bonus one taken on the attractor. Two naturals imitating two different stages of a hatch, such as a dun on the surface and an emerging dun, cover the odds. During concentrations of insects, such as green beetles, two flies are better than one for visibility. Having one on the surface and another just below will cover more options — say, one imitating a dead beetle and the other a moving one. Combinations of nymphs or small wet flies can also increase the numbers of fish rising to the dry fly and the dry fly makes a reasonable indicator. Tie patterns with bright coloured wings for daytime use and dark wings for low light if you are having problems seeing the dry fly, instead of using larger patterns.

Presentation is the third key to successful dry fly fishing. Most presentations require a natural drag-free drift, as this copies the natural insect most of the time and does not disturb the water surface, which can scare the trout. For long drifts down foam lines or along bank side vegetation, mend the line and keep some slack in the flyline and leader to prevent drag. As the drift starts to go downstream, mend so the dry fly goes downstream first and feed slack as it progresses. This will greatly extend the drift and enable placement of the fly under trees or into snaggy areas.

Dry fly fishing fast water requires short leaders and short drifts. Keep the whole rig well coated in floatant to reduce the chance of the fly being dragged under by the turbulent water and mend quickly and often.

When stalking trout, false cast to the side until all water is flicked off and drop the fly at the upstream end of the trout's window of visibility. This is dictated by how deep it is — the deeper, the longer the visibility. Casting beyond this often results in the trout failing to see the fly, or it sees it too late, resulting in a chased fly and obvious results. Dropping the fly at the edge of the trout's window seems to catch its attention without suspicion and gives the trout time to take the fly in a confident manner. Dry flies are ideal for fishing downstream into tight areas, or to trout lying above obstacles. Start with the rod upstream and the line and fly downstream, then manoeuvre everything into the desired current and point the rod downstream as the fly drifts downstream. Feed plenty of slack throughout the drift and then skitter the fly across the surface at the end of the drift. When a trout rises to the fly, let it go back under, then smoothly lift the rod until the trout is felt — then give a firm tug to set the hook.

Stillwater dry fly fishing success requires patience and careful observation before casting. Do not grease the leader because it's desirable to have the nylon below the surface giving out less shadow and surface disturbance. Drop the fly well ahead of the trout, in its path, but preferably where it, and not the flyline and leader, will be visible — such as along weed edges, shadow edges, among float debris, or when the surface is disturbed by the trout, wind, or rain. Dropping the fly on the trout's tail often results in the trout quickly turning around and aggressively taking the fly. A sinking dry fly, or one twitched occasionally, will work well. Trout cruising popular lake shorelines can become very educated. But two tricks are always worth trying. One is to present the fly on the lake side, rather than the shore side. The other is to use a sinking line and long leader to remove any line shadow and surface disturbance.

Knowing when to strike after the trout has taken your dry fly is a topic of considerable debate. Some anglers count to three before striking, while others raise the rod smoothly as soon as the fish goes down. There is no firm rule. Strike to suit the situation.

A slow rise will require a count to three. Fast rises warrant a strike as soon as the fish disappears. Large fish, especially browns, generally require a longer hesitation before striking. Rainbows and small fish require a shorter hesitation. Small patterns only need to slide into the trout's jaw to hook up, whereas large patterns will require a firmer strike.

Fishing cicadas is a specialist activity in terms of dry fly fishing. These insects hatch during the summer, often in huge numbers. Creating a deafening noise as the male chirps to attract a mate. Several species exist, with colours varying from black, to green, to brown. Trout love cicadas and normally secretive large fish will aggressively rise to them. Trout have an interesting way of taking cicadas. They often track the fly before taking it in what can only be described as explosive rises. I have watched trout either let the fly drift past then suddenly attack it, or tilt back until vertical then smash it. I have also seen trout drown the fly first before taking it.

Large attractor patterns, stimulating movement and air bubbles on the cicada's body, work the best in rivers. In stillwater, use natural imitations. On rivers, drift the fly along tree-lined banks, foam lines, and in the shadows, especially on the windward side. On lake shorelines, have the wind behind and drift the fly over the weedbeds and dropoffs. If in a boat, drift with the wind, using a sea anchor. Double rigged cicada patterns are very effective, as is a heavy, splashy presentation. Cicadas are ideal to drift downstream under vegetation and into snaggy places that cannot be fished from below. Simply drag the fly across and out of these areas and expect heavy takes. Windy or rainy days flush lots of dying cicadas into the water, resulting in some outrageous fishing as trout gorge themselves. Cicada season is a great time to driftboat rivers and bang dry flies into the gaps among the trees.

Green manuka beetles appear in late spring in high numbers. Trout feed heavily on these, especially in backcountry areas. But trout taking green beetles can be difficult to catch because they seem to concentrate on live ones still moving, or those that are sinking. Using patterns that copy this will work best, or cast the fly right into the fish's path or feeding lane to trigger a reaction. In stillwater, try using a sinking line with a light leader and a foam body beetle pattern that floats well.

Suspend this beetle just below the water surface and give it a slight twitch just as a trout approaches.

Caddis flies typically hatch just on dark in cloudy, warm, humid conditions. The pupa streaks to the surface, pops out, and runs across the water surface to hide in the vegetation. Trout can be heard loudly pursuing the caddis. Drag-free drifts do not work here. To a stout 3m leader, attach a #12 to #8 caddis pattern that floats well and creates a wake. Deer hair body patterns are ideal. Add 1m of tippet and tie on a small wet fly pattern. Position above the trout and cast across and slightly down the current, retaining a short loop of flyline between the reel and finger on the rod handle. Follow the swing of the line with the rod and lower the tip as it comes across current to your side of the river. If a take is felt, drop the loop and calmly raise the rod, allowing the hooked trout to take line. If nothing happens at the end of the swing, twitch the fly in several metres and re-cast. If you cannot get above trout chasing caddis, cast upstream to them and smoothly lift the rod, dragging the fly across the surface, then re-cast. Lake outlets and lowland rivers are the best places for caddis, but they are prolific in all waters.

Backcountry rocky rivers hold huge numbers of stoneflies. Most of the winged adults walk out of the water to hatch, but the smaller black ones hatch on the water's surface and skitter across to the bank. High floating black patterns work best presented normally to prevent the trout seeing the angler in the often clear waters. Sometimes, though, trout become selective, targeting the ones skittering on the surface. Cast down and across, then drift the fly into likely trout holding spots and skitter the fly across the surface.

Trout love willow grubs, which live inside those reddish blemishes on willow tree leaves. The little lemon yellow coloured grub hatches in the summer and often falls into the water. Trout line up in the feeding lanes below willow trees and quietly rise to grubs wiggling in the surface film. Sounds like an easy situation to catch lots of trout. Unfortunately, trout key on the wiggling grub, which is impossible to imitate. Good success can be had with an accurate imitation cast right on the trout's nose, or an attractor pattern will get its share. A double rig, with a willow grub copy and a small Royal Wulff works for me.

Damsel flies are always present when fishing stillwater fisheries, but the winged adult does not attract many trout until it lays eggs and starts to die. A pattern, which lies flat in the surface film and simulates the dying, fluttering wings of the insect, will quickly be eaten. Drift the fly off the end of reeds, raupo, and sticks where trout, especially brownies, will be patrolling.

Adult mayflies, also known as spinners, die after laying eggs on the water surface. They drift downstream in large numbers, providing great dry fly fishing opportunities. Spent spinners will concentrate in foam lines, backwaters, and wind will blow them along one bank. Patterns that copy size, colour, and the sparkling, clear wings of the spinner lying flat on the water surface are the best to use. By casting when the trout is back below the surface checking out the next mouthful, the imitation will catch its attention more quickly. The days after good hatch conditions are the best and will result in some of the best dry fly fishing. Many times I have seen trout lined up along the bank literally hoovering dozens of spent spinners concentrated in a foam line, or pushed along the bank by the wind.

Mouse plagues regularly happen in New Zealand and mice are around in varying numbers all the time. Brown trout love them and fishing a mouse pattern is interesting and mainly conducted at night. Check out the area of lake or river during the day and return well after dark. A large deer hair mouse pattern on a strong leader is then cast out and retrieved in an enticing, non-stop way. On moving water, cast across and upstream to retrieve across and down, just like a real mouse would swim across a river. The take is usually loud and dramatic, often right under the rod tip. Raise the rod firmly to set the large hook and look out. If you have located a monster brown trout and cannot fool him during the day, try a mouse at night. It will test even the calmest of nerves.

Other dry fly fishing opportunities than discussed here abound. Lace moths, bees, brown beetles, and ants are a few of the terrestrial insects that trout regularly feed on, not to mention all the different mayflies that live in our streams. Learn when and where all these insects feature in a trout's diet and a well-presented dry fly will provide a lifetime of angling fun and help satisfy an insatiable addiction.

Of Trout And Clouds Of Bugs

BY ZANE MIRFIN

Montana's Missouri River shone like a giant silver mirror in the hot morning sun. Overlooking the meandering river from a high roadside bank, the green vegetation near the water contrasted sharply with the parched dry upland pastures and terraces. Over the water, huge clouds of tiny bugs, hundreds of metres long, pirouetted like ballerinas in a final mating dance. More importantly in this world class tailwater, trout were rising everywhere — hundreds of them. Scrambling into waders, we hurried down the bank with our broken down rods, shivering in anticipation of the sport ahead.

The water was covered with thousands of dead and dying trico spinners and literally was boiling with rising, slashing, and tailing brown and rainbow trout. Great pods of fish were up on the surface offering dozens of targets to cast at from the one position. Our tiny #22 imitations disappeared into the chemical soup of life on the river's surface and the trout were not so easily fooled. Repeated accurate casting with 7x tippet finally hooked the first fish, but it was frustrating fishing. Finally in desperation, I tried a pair of #16 nymphs fished just under the surface. Bingo, I had discovered the magic formula and the fishing became easy. There was just too much food on the surface and the subsurface nymphs were just too tempting as they drifted over schools of hungry trout. Then an hour or so later, as suddenly as it had all begun, the feeding melee was over. The huge river flowed placid and serene, the surface unbroken as if there had never been a fish alive in the water. As anglers we all dream of angling situations like this with mass hatches and abundant rising fish. Here in New Zealand, we probably can't compete with some of the better western American tailwater fisheries in terms of insect abundance or trout numbers per mile. But we have many important lowland waterways that turn on some pretty impressive fishing under ideal circumstances. These are generally larger rivers with stable bottoms and high fish densities. They are generally close to home and have easy access. The fish may not be huge, but will mostly run 1–4lb with the possibility of a trophy never far away. These rivers are highly valued by anglers and sustain heavy usage due to the high catch rate and easy access.

In the northern South Island, main-stem rivers, such as the lower Motueka, Pelorus, and Wairau, are good examples. But the Manawatu, or Tukituki in the North Island, the West Coast's Arnold, or the Mataura in Southland are other examples. Such rivers flow through agricultural settings and are often extensively modified, but valuable to anglers because of the access values and the high trout populations. The key characteristic of such rivers is that all hold large biomasses of aquatic insects — the key to trout production. If the bugs find a river to their liking, then trout will flourish too. However, that is not to say that the fishing will always be easy!

It has often been said that 90% of trout are caught by 10% of the anglers and this ratio may even be understated. Even on rivers such as the Motueka, regularly cited as New Zealand's most heavily stocked river (often 300 to 400+ fish per kilometre), many anglers regularly go home without success. Not catching fish is a stressful experience and the consistently successful anglers have unlocked the secrets of the trout's world that normally revolves around food, temperature, barometric pressure, and sex.

Being able to anticipate when, where, and what fish are likely to eat in these lowland fisheries is the secret to success. These rivers are what I like to call "hatch-driven" fisheries, where fish activity almost always revolves around food availability.

In headwater rivers and semi-sterile rivers with less diverse insect populations, it is often easier to catch fish because they will usually eat what comes their way with less regard for moon phase, barometric pressure, or even water temperature. In such headwater fisheries, it is often possible to at least catch a few fish even though circumstances may not be ideal. Sure, headwater fish respond to hatches too, but such hatches are of lesser importance in the ability of anglers to catch fish. Hatch-driven fisheries in contrast can often seem like a watery morgue in non-feeding periods when you could swear there wasn't a fish alive in the river. Whipping the water to a foam with your flies is mostly a waste of time in such circumstances because if they aren't eating you generally can't catch them!

Hatch-driven fisheries are often all go — where the fishing is hot, hot, hot, or stone-cold useless. Figuring out when to fish is probably more important than knowing with what to fish. I find hatch-driven fisheries hard going during periods of inclement weather, or when the barometer is dropping like a stone. Once the storm breaks and the rain starts, fish will begin to feed. However given a choice, the ideal conditions are a bluebird sunny day with a large anticyclone sitting over the country bringing high barometric pressure. Such conditions are pleasant for the angler and conducive to the insects and thus the trout.

Trout in lowland rivers will feed all day, but definite feeding cycles are very discernable. When you catch one trout, you will normally catch others soon after. Some days you just need to keep fishing until they turn on. Other days you will be wasting your time from the start.

Think carefully. Remember, the human brain is the most powerful fishing tool known to man. Think and catch fish! Is the water too cold? Is the water too warm? This is where you will need a thermometer to test things. It is well known that the optimum temperature for trout feeding activity (and insect movement too) is between about 13–18°C. This means in winter, early season, and late autumn that afternoons may be the best time to fish, as water temperatures warm up and cold-blooded critters start moving. Conversely in summer, mornings and evenings may offer the best feeding conditions for trout, as water temperatures rise to uncomfortable temperatures during the peak sun hours, then cool again as darkness approaches.

If you're on the water and want to fish despite the water being a tad too cool, try fishing slower, deeper water that trout drop back into to save energy. If the water is really heating up, fish fast, highly oxygenated, often shallow ripples that fish will move into to feed during the height of summer. These rules aren't hard and fast so just keep experimenting until you strike the magic formula and meet with success. Sometimes it can be a good idea to fish the main river during the morning and retreat to a cooler tributary or stream mouths during hot summer afternoons. During colder periods or overcast days, try this in reverse.

Although angling pressure can be heavy on lowland fisheries with good fish populations, it pays to block other anglers out of your mind and out of the angling equation. Fish are either feeding, or they're not. Many is the time customers and friends under my supervision have fished up behind someone, or we have found out a run was fished earlier in the day by another angler, but we still had greater success than they did. They weren't doing anything different fishing-wise — the only difference being that the fish were feeding when we were there. This has happened in reverse many times also! Mentally block out any boot prints in the sand — the odds are often on your side. Sometimes you can actually think too much when fishing! In my opinion, heavy angling pressure can actually make fish easier to catch, as it can push fish into certain pieces of water where they are more susceptible to capture.

Lowland fisheries were made to be fished blind. By blind fishing, I don't mean "chuck and chance" fishing, but rather select-ively fishing targeted pieces of water in the expectation that you will catch fish. If you can see feeding fish, then great, catch them. If you can't see feeding fish, then don't assume they aren't there. Don't be afraid to throw plenty of casts into difficult-to-see places. You'll be surprised what you catch. Also, just because you think you can see into a run doesn't mean that there are no fish there either. Lowland rivers often have algal growth on the stones and such rivers can be very difficult to spot fish. Smaller trout are often beautifully camouflaged against the bottom stratum and rainbows in fast flows can be the very devil to spot.

If in doubt, throw a few casts in there. Remember, early and late in the season and in winter fishing locations, that low sun angle is not going to assist sight fishing, so the majority of fish caught on lowland rivers will be caught fishing blind.

Late April, two years ago, saw me guiding on the middle Motueka with a lovely American couple of modest fishing ability. It was a short day throwing small nymphs, but the fish were on. They hooked 40 to 50 fish for the day (we lost count) and I never spotted a trout all day! Having said that, I'd hate to admit how many times I've flogged "the Mot" into oblivion, hoping and praying that one measly trout would eat the fly. The moral here is that you can't catch trout sitting at home.

Now we get onto the fun part. The bugs themselves! Lowland hatch-driven fisheries have a magic potpourri of insect life, a huge melting pot of all sorts of fascinating beasties that have inspired anglers and flytiers since before Walton (BW).

You'd be a sad human being if you didn't get excited about a blister hatch of mayfly duns pouring off the water during a sunny afternoon and watching a pod of black heads rhythmically harvesting the bounty. Watch for birds, such as swallows and chaffinches, working the water while fishing. It is often the precursor of fun times ahead. Any small dry fly will probably work, but a small Adams or Parachute Adams is just the ticket.

Late season mayfly hatches are a feature of many rivers. Around Anzac Day in April is a fun time to fish the rivers of Southland. Standing on the banks of the Mataura with small may fly duns pouring off the water, it is not difficult to appreciate what great fishing resources we have available in New Zealand.

Hatch-driven fish are noted for their selective feeding. They often will lock onto specific food items that require quite specific imitation at times. Sometimes they will be concentrating on

Elevation makes spotting trout easier [PHOTO: DAVID HALLETT]

It pays to take the fight to a fish, even on small streams

[PHOTO: DAVID HALLETT]

Keep the rod tip high when fighting a fish [PHOTO: DAVID HALLETT]

Rivers, like the Rough, can turn on the fish while clearing from floods [PHOTO: DAVID HALLETT]

Drifting is a great way to cover lots of water [PHOTO: DAVID HALLETT]

Working the lake shallows [PHOTO: DAVID HALLETT]

Fly selection is crucial to success [PHOTO: KRIS SHEPHERD]

Deep in the Wangapeka
[PHOTO: DAVID HALLETT]

specific life phases of a particular insect type and may ignore a high floating dry, but inhale an emerger or spinner. This skill factor in picking the rises and choosing an appropriate imitation is what makes fishing fun.

Imitation size is possibly the most important criterion in fishing lowland hatch-driven fisheries. Because fish are spoiled for choice with an abundance of food, they will often lock onto a certain size insect and ignore everything else. Most anglers fish with flies that are too large. I regularly fish with flies down to #20. A size #16 Pheasant Tail is my standard nymph and is a deadly fly on any lowland river. If nymph fishing faster water, try using a heavy sinker fly, or attach some split shot to get your small nymphs down into the bingo zone. Fish aren't going to move a long way for a small bug, so sometimes it will take a few presentations before they see the fly and make the decision to eat it. Nymph fishing is a great way to catch fish and fill in time between non-hatch periods, but you just can't beat fishing to visible fish on the surface.

Evening caddis hatches can be very exciting, either fishing dries to slashing trout or swinging a pair of wet flies down and across. Don't forget about stripping a Woolly Bugger, or such like, after dark through some of the big pools where lunkers may reside. Every year double digit fish are taken out of heavily fished public water by diligent anglers fishing after dark. One trick that used to work well in the States, and works well here, is to fish an Elk Hair Caddis dry fly when you first get to the river in the morning during summer. If it was a nice evening the day before, the odds are that there was a caddis hatch, and the trout in lowland rivers are always on the lookout for caddis stragglers from the night before.

Spent caddis and spent mayfly spinners are commonly encountered on hatch-driven fisheries. The lower Wairau, is a magic spent spinner river during summer. Some pools can literally be dotted with small black heads pock-marking the water as they sip many mouthfuls per minute. The best time to encounter spent rusty spinners is in the morning when the dead and dying insects are in the water en masse after a night of mating. Use small flies and light tippets and be on the river early before the coastal upstream sea breezes begin around mid-morning or lunch time, depending on the day. This is a familiar weather pattern on many lowland rivers during the warm summer months. Often you will see a small head suck down your fly, but when you tighten up you will feel the weight of a silver bullet fresh from the sea that will rip you into your backing and may pull your scales down as far as 4kg. The Wairau is just that kind of river!

Terrestrials are another major summer food source that can offer frustratingly satisfying fishing opportunities. Fish can become very selective when feeding on willow grubs beneath overhanging willow trees. Tight casting and healthy fish feeding right on the surface can really elevate the blood pressure. I find the best strategy is to fish a sunken willow grub imitation on light tippet and twitch it when it approaches the trout. The downside to this is that it is very easy to bust off fish.

Passion Vine Hoppers are another local specialty and can be very difficult to imitate consistently. I remember one great day fishing with angling doyen Norman Marsh unsolving the riddle of the Passion Vine Hoppers. Norman had invited me out to fish the hatch after we had both been involved in assisting Fish & Game with the 1990 Motueka Water Conservation Order submissions. A bluebird day, with low river flows and lots of rising fish set the scene for an educational day. Norman had some secret, difficult to reach banks that he lowered himself down on an old tow rope from the back of my truck. Norman held his rod in his teeth, his golden Labrador dog under one arm, and the rope in his other hand! It was a great experience watching the master at work -- Norman patiently watching the rising fish working, waiting for the right time in the fish's feeding rhythm to throw the delicately tied lacewing. Then the soft slurp and the slow lift to impale the trout on the hook. Norman taught me many things that day and most of them didn't have a lot to do with fishing.

There are tons of other terrestrial insects that can be seasonally important on lowland waters, ranging from cicadas, beetles, and ants back through to other aquatic insects such as midges, craneflies, and even stoneflies. Make sure you have a well-stocked flybox because you never know what you may encounter, even on a stream you know very well.

Two Octobers ago saw me standing on the banks of Otago's Taieri River, a tannin-coloured sinuous marvel of nature. Fishing had been challenging, but on this day my two friends and I stood quietly beside the flooded backwater that Ranfurly guide, Dean Whaanga, had directed us to. It was freezing standing in the swirling daylight mist, our feet frozen in our chest waders, the river and backwater limpid and barren. We discussed heading back to Dean's place to warm up, but decided to wait out our last chance on the Taieri. After what seemed like several hours, we hadn't even made a cast when suddenly it happened. Large grey midges started pouring off the water as trout came from nowhere, swirling and slurping in the surface film. For about an hour we could do no wrong -- two dozen fat Taieri browns up to 2.7kg hooked. Then as suddenly as it started, the hatch tapered off, the trout disappeared, and the river flowed serene.

Lowland hatch-driven fisheries offer many different facets to anglers. They are a resource under pressure from humanity, insatiable in its desire for irrigation water, hydro electric generation, dairy farm development, and lifestyle blocks. They offer anglers refuge close to urban areas, excitement after work, and respite from the chores of domesticity. When the pressures of daily life get too much, I find myself thinking about standing in a favourite lowland river with yellow autumn leaves in profusion, roaring stags patrolling adjacent paddocks, and orange-sided brownies taking with fierce aggression. There's just nothing else like it.

Making Pocket Water Productive

BY TONY ENTWISTLE

Noted American angler, Nick Lyons, neatly sum-marises the essence of pocket water fishing: "Pocket water has its special delights. It's not 'exact imitation' and much of it is coarse and close, not fine and far. You are looking for likely water mostly, seeking a place a trout would seek, where it can get food and safety. You are watching a vibrantly alive surface, braided with twisting currents and swirls and bubbles and eddies. You are looking for a patch of water a couple of feet around, and you have to make quick decisions to get your fly above it, so the fly will float into the pocket. You move quickly because you probably need only put a fly across a pocket a half dozen times to know if a fish will take it. Floats are brief, strikes are quick."

In the strictest sense, pocket water is the small area of water between obstacles, where the main flow of a river has been inter-rupted. Most commonly the obstructions are large rocks and boulders, but logs and basement rock structures also create great pocket water. While pocket water may be found anywhere in a river system, it is more likely in the steeper, upper reaches.

Most good pocket water looks like an impossible mosaic of violent movement, a maelstrom of white foam and surging chutes, accompanied by an all encompassing symphony of thunder. Why would anyone want to fish it? Because trout sometimes love it!

The best pocket water is a happy accident of ideal conditions that suit and support good numbers of trout at the right time of year. Often pocket water holds large numbers of mid-sized trout, which will be well conditioned, fighting fit, and eager to take a fly. It's not normally regarded as big fish water, but expect the unexpected.

Many anglers avoid this style of angling simply because understanding pocket water and how to fish it looks like too much trouble. That's a pity! Pocket water will test your stamina, wading ability, and fishing skills.

Productive areas of pocket water will feature good pools or deep runs either above or below, which provide good holding water where trout move in times of very high or low flow or colder water temperatures. Most often it occurs in a tight spot in a river and usually marks a change in the river's gradient. Seldom is good water found contained within tight rock-walled gorges where the full power of the river is concentrated during high flows, or in places that don't see good summer light at least part of the day.

The best pocket water concentrates the essentials in a trout's life. Usually it is summer trout water, reflecting an increase in water temperature, higher midday sun, and lower river levels. Lower water levels and increased insect activity may see pocket water action as early as mid-November, but best fishing will be over by mid-March.

Good pocket water is usually insect rich and features a large number of prime lies where trout are able to feed, rest and maintain security with the minimum of effort. A good stretch might look quite devastating and too violent to hold any fish at all, but the average water velocity throughout will actually be slower than many other areas in a river. A great deal of the water's velocity is reversed in the pressure waves in front of rocks, the upward motion in standing waves and the back eddies behind every rock. In fact, pocket water can be a cushy place for trout to live – a series of mini pools and food rich havens.

Pocket water may curiously require minimum effort from trout, but any angler seeking these trout is contemplating fishing that will demand much physical fitness, fly and line management skills, quick reactions and lots of imagination.

So where do trout lie in pocket water, and how best should we attack them? Traditionally in New Zealand, we approach our fish from downstream. Much of our technique is based on English dead drift, dry fly and small nymph techniques, which adopted the downstream/upstream approach. Much of our water is very clear by world standards as well, so approaching from downstream keeps us from the trout's view for longer. Also significant for many of our wild trout is their acute sense of smell and adverse reaction to human scent throughout the day.

Think of pocket water as a boisterous ladder of small pools. Tackle one step at a time, each pocket on its own merits, looking at the parts and not the whole, moving forward and upward.

Many anglers around my area enjoy stalking and spotting trout. This style of fishing suits the nature of our largely resident brown populations and is both absorbing and highly skilful. Yet most anglers would do better to use their imaginations and have greater faith in their own judgment of where trout should be. This is especially so when fishing pocket water. When spotting conditions are not ideal, anglers needn't try to confirm every fish by seeing it first. Try drifting a cast or two into the areas where you are expecting to see a trout.

Long casts are not practicable. But anglers should still follow the principle of trying to cover as much water as is possible on each drift. Once you put the fly out, some form of line control and management is needed to ensure a good drift to cover fish. This may entail laying the cast out with some slack and also mending it several times as it drifts back downstream. Whatever, the effectiveness of the drift will be over the moment the line begins to drag on the fly.

A drag-free drift is the ultimate aim. The more regularly you achieve it, the better your overall catch rate. The how-to will vary considerably between situations. Anglers will be more successful in pocket water when they learn to apply different casts, including curve casts, tuck casts, pile casts, roll casts, reach casts, slack line casts, and aerial mends.

When you first perceive drag, lift off and re-cast. Drifts may be very short, maybe as short as only a metre or two. The theory is to make the first cast and drift the best, as this is the most likely to take a fish. Any subsequent casts will rely on the state of awareness, patience, or nerve of the trout to remain potentially catchable. If the pocket is small, the angler should go for broke right away and try to cover the fish.

Most pocket water situations can be tackled applying some imagination and judgment. There will be many variations on a theme, but always the principle remains — you must judge where best to put that first cast for maximum effect.

Dry fly fishing in pocket water can be exciting and productive when the trout are focussed. Seldom is there a need to resort to small imitative patterns as generally bigger attractor patterns, such as Royal Wulffs, Humpies, hoppers, and cicadas, produce vigorous and unsubtle takes.

I most often fish with weighted nymphs and will change to a dry whenever I see a fish taking off the top. Two weighted nymphs work better than one and when legally allowed to add weight to the leader, I often add a small split shot or a twist of soft lead to speed their descent.

Great pocket water patterns for browns include the Buller Caddis, Nelson Brown, Carty's Coloburiscus, Green Stonefly (up to early January), various gold bead head patterns, rubber legs, and, of course, the ubiquitous Hare & Copper. All tend to suggest life in a nymph rather than strictly imitate specific insects, and this is the key to a successful pocket water nymph.

Because trout are not always seen, detecting when a trout has taken a fly will be difficult. Watching for the end of the flyline to stop works some of the time, but can be limiting. I usually make use of a small woollen indicator, seldom bigger than the wings of a #10 Royal Wulff. An indicator gives positive indication of a take and helps in judging drift and drag.

There is only a split second to make a strike. It doesn't require a savage movement to set a small hook, but judgment and confidence to react to a moment in time.

Other ways to attack pocket water exist. Downstreaming with

a nymph or wet fly pattern, worked on either a sink tip or sinking line can be very productive, although in water with very big rocks the sinking line can be a curse. Europeans employ a technique called "short-lining", which can be deadly and is relevant to fishing deep pocket water. It involves using a short line and heavily weighted nymphs. The angler barely casts any distance, holds a high rod, and stands in close to the pocket being fished. The nymph or nymphs are then worked, like deep dapping, through the prime lies. It works well in turbid water, especially on European grayling, which favour holding in numbers in the eddy behind a rock. I have used it with success in some of our deeper, heavier pocket water where dead drifting a nymph simply won't achieve the required depth because the line and leader are working against extreme drag and turbulence.

Like all forms of fishing, getting the best out of pocket water is as much a matter of attitude as it is hard and fast rules.

Mastering Difficult Trout

BY ROSS MILLICHAMP

An angler is walking up a South Island high country stream in early summer. The holiday season has yet to arrive and the trout should be undisturbed. The angler does not bother looking into the rough water where fish are hard to spot. It is not until he reaches a pretty pool that he slows down and starts to peer into the water. At the bottom of the pool, the streambed is littered with large boulders, which have been brought down from the headwaters in floods. Here the angler tries his best, but cannot avoid scaring the pair of fat trout that are perfectly camouflaged against the mottled stream bottom. The angler shrugs his shoulders, but he is not overly concerned, as he knows that the best part of the pool is still to come. Right at the head of the pool is a narrow piece of water known as the "eye". The water of the eye is calm but lies immediately adjacent to the fast water, which drains the upstream rapid. As expected, the angler easily spots the dark waving form of a trout starkly contrasted against the light coloured, fine shingle that typically collects at the head of the pool. The fish is sitting in the calm water, but it's ducking out into the current from time to time to intercept some of the abundant insect drift it carries. The angler selects a big, bushy nymph and lobs it into the fast water upstream of the trout. The fast current keeps the line, leader, and fly in a straight line and creates the perfect drag-free drift. The take is easy to see when it comes — the angler's bright orange flyline lurches to the left and dives under the surface. The angler lifts his rod, sets the hook, and before long has his first of the day under his belt.

Sadly, this scene is becoming a thing of the past. Our high country fisheries are still in great shape because their catchments are generally protected from development by conservative land management practices. What has changed is the amount of angler pressure these catchments are subject to. The chances of an angler coming across a naive trout at the top of a pretty pool are becoming remote. And difficult, obstinate trout are becoming the norm. Another tradition that is fast becoming a thing of the past is the adage that the further upstream you go, the less disturbed the fish will be. These days the upper reaches can he among the most heavily fished due to the presence of helicopter-bound anglers.

Trout are not born with inbuilt defences against anglers. The education occurs over time — the more anglers they encounter, the faster they learn. In very heavily fished waters, it would be easy to believe that the trout become almost uncatchable. However, the one thing in the angler's favour is the number of insects the typical trout has to consume each day to stay alive and grow. Irrespective of angler pressure, trout have to spend a large proportion of their day plucking insects from the drift. As long as the trout does not suspect the angler's presence and is presented with a fly that drifts naturally and closely resembles its natural prey, there is no reason why it will not respond. This is the challenge you must overcome to catch difficult trout.

The typical South Island trout stream opens for the season with a bit of a flurry. Although the trout population may not be at its peak, the fact that they have not been fished to for five months means that trout can be easy pickings. Over the next few months, the fishing should hold its own, as new trout migrate up from the lower reaches and increasing water temperatures lead to increased periods of trout activity. However by mid-summer, the tracks leading up the river become deeper and the trout become more difficult. At this stage of the season, the very worst thing you can do is follow another party up the river, no matter what tricks you have up your sleeve. Thankfully, it is quite easy to avoid this scenario by rising early and getting to the river before the sun hits the water. Even if you do run into another party on arrival, they will not have started fishing and should be amicable to a water-sharing arrangement.

In order to get really good fishing, you need to fish water that has been rested for three or four days. This is more difficult unless you have a friendly farmer who will keep an eye on comings and goings. One way to be certain of fishing undisturbed water is to adopt the salmon angler's habit of fishing the river the first day it is fishable after a fresh. Another is to go out on the first calm day after a string of rough ones. As mentioned above, the days of only having to look at the head of the pool for trout are over. This water still attracts fish because it offers shelter in close proximity to a good food supply. However, chances are that the trout that choose to sit here are likely to have encountered a lot more anglers than the trout that sit in places where they are difficult to spot. The low density of trout in many New Zealand waters means that looking into every piece of water is not the answer. If you do not bypass unlikely water, you will not cover enough ground to come across many fish. The best answer is to learn the river so that you learn which water to look into and which water to ignore.

Movement is the main thing that scares trout. The less of your body that is exposed, the less chance you have of scaring fish. Make use of any riverside vegetation, much the same as you would when stalking an animal. If there is no vegetation, stand well back from the bank so that only your upper body is visible to the trout. Most important of all is to slow down when approaching water that is likely to hold trout.

Glare is one of the main frustrations faced by anglers trying to spot trout. Unfortunately, the glare is at its worst when the angler looks directly upstream. It is very tempting to look across the current where the glare is less and the trout easier to see. In order to catch difficult trout, you need to resist this temptation and concentrate on looking upstream. If the glare is so bad that you must look across the current, stand as far back from the bank as you can.

Make a mental note of where it is and where you intend to land your fly. Duck down out of view, sneak back downstream to a good casting position, and commence battle.

The further away the trout is when you spot it, the less disturbed it will be and the more likely it is to respond to your fly. Chances are that if you do not spot the trout until you can see its whole form clearly, you are too close. Peer into the water that is at the extreme end of your vision and stop as soon as you can see any irregular, shape or colour that could be a fish. Stare at the shape until you are either completely sure that it is, or is not a fish. If you remain unsure, treat it as a fish and have a cast. In some cases, there is no way to tell if a shape is a fish unless you get so close that you will scare it.

In order to catch difficult trout, you need to use flies that closely resemble insects in the drift. This rules out flies such as the #10 Hare & Copper, which is deliberately made to be bigger and bulkier than most aquatic insects. Flies such as this act as "attractor" patterns to cause trout to take them in preference to the other insects in the drift. Next time you are on your favourite trout stream, turn over a few rocks and pick up a typical mayfly. Now take a look through the nymphs in your flybox and find one that is a similar size to the mayfly. Chances are you will be looking at a #14 or #16 fly. The problem with using small nymphs is that it is difficult to sink them to the depths where trout may be lying. The introduction of tungsten beads to the flytiers arsenal has helped greatly here, with flies as small as #14 being able to be sunk to depths that were previously the preserves of #10s and #12s.

The only fault in this argument is the puzzling habit of difficult brown trout that show rude indifference to a well-presented #14 nymph, but greedily inhale a #8 dry! For some reason, big dry flies often trigger recalcitrant trout into activity, especially in high country areas where large terrestrial insects fall into the water at regular intervals. Even more puzzling is that trout respond better when the big fly hits the water with a splash than they do to a gentle touch down.

Choosing the correct leader is also of vital importance. Tradition suggests that as the trout get more difficult, you should use a longer and lighter leader. I agree with this tradition, but only to a point. Never use a leader longer than you are able to cast well. A good presentation with a short leader always beats a poor presentation with a long one. Most anglers using modern flyrods can cast a long leader in calm conditions, but struggle when the wind gets up. Cut the leader back until you can cast it well.

The biggest secret to catching difficult trout is the quality of the first presentation. Unless your trout is in deep water, the end of the flyline should land just behind the fish, while the leader carries the fly three to four metres above. The moment the flyline hits the water is when you have the greatest chance of scaring the fish. If the water is very smooth and calm, or if you are casting to a fish in shallow water, you will not get away with landing even the leader on top of it. You are better to cast half a metre to the side and hope that the fish will move to take the fly. If you intend to cast to one side of the fish, make it on the outside of the fish. The faster water is more likely to hide the cast and fish tend to look toward the faster water for food. If the fish is away from the bank, you can cast; from slightly side on, so that neither the flyline nor leader splashes down on top of the fish, but the fly will drift right to it.

Keep false casts to a minimum and avoid making them over fish. The main purpose of false casts is to get enough line out through the rings to load the rod for the final shoot. An alternative way to load the rod is to let five metres of line stream out in the current below you. Lift the line into the air, make one false cast out to the side of the fish, and then make the delivery cast. Any more than one false cast is excessive and likely to scare fish. The longer the final shoot can be made while still being accurate, the less chance you have of scaring the fish.

If you are in doubt as to whether to use a nymph or dry fly, use the dry, as it is less likely to scare the fish. If the first drift is good but is ignored by the trout, change your fly. Never make more than two good presentations to a trout with the same fly. Changing the fly does two things. It gives the trout a look at another pattern or size, and it gives the fish a rest while you are changing. The only time you should persevere with the same fly for a number of casts is when fishing to trout in deep water. Here it is difficult to be certain that the trout has actually seen the fly. If it fails to respond to what you think is a good drift, try casting further upstream to give the nymph more chance to sink. Gradually increase the size and weight of the fly until you are certain that the fish has seen it. It is quite unusual to catch a deep water trout on the first couple of casts. Most often it takes time to work out the correct amount of weight to use and where to cast to bring the fly into the trout's field of view.

The final thing to know is when to give up! Difficult trout have a nasty habit of not flushing when they know you are there and you can waste an awful lot of time fishing to them. Do not spend a lot of time casting to fish lying still on the bottom. Once you are sure you have made a couple of good drifts with three or four different flies, move on and try to find another.

The Magic Of Uncertainty

BY TONY ENTWISTLE

Undoubtedly, big rivers present a daunting prospect for most anglers compared to the intimate nature of small streams. They have strength of character, impose barriers, and command respect, confronting us with varying degrees of intimidation, both physical and psychological. But while big waters may challenge anglers physically and emotionally and demand a wider range of skills, mixed with their magic of uncertainty, they also provide great opportunity. Whatever it is that trout like or need, it is often found in greater volume on big rivers.

So at what point does a river become big? Simple measurement of width and volumetric flow is somehow too arbitrary and inadequate, although a big river will be one that most of us can't cast across and won't be easily crossed on foot, if at all.

Writing about Oregon's famous Deschutes River in *The Habit of Rivers* (1994), Ted Leeson, captures the essence of what makes a river big: "...nor does the river even approximate my platonic trout stream. The size and depth, the forbidding velocity of the current, the sheer volume of water, all exceed the proportions of comfortable imagining, and much of what is there seems beyond reach or rapport. You can become familiar with the river, but it defies the intimacy of my ideal. Yet the place is magnetic for precisely this reason: It confronts you with your own incapacity to know."

While many of New Zealand's trout streams are not "as big" on the world scale of rivers, we are blessed with plenty that engage the essence of big water, whether through sheer scale, the width of their beds, or the force of flow. Fishing big waters presents very real problems of scale, access, and technique, often compounded by genuine danger to one's person, and until you've spent time on specific waters, it's tough to get an overview of what confronts you?

If, as Leeson puts it, big water promotes "incapacity to know", this might explain the dearth of angling literature on how to approach flyfishing in big rivers (salmon and steelhead aside). Most angling authors prefer not to confront their incapacities and may well be just as intimidated by big rivers as mere fishing mortals.

Firstly, a broad overview of the river is needed to narrow down the options and some simple things are worth doing that will minimise the legwork. Topographic maps, or aerial photographs are very helpful and will soon become essential equipment, if an angler plans to fish more than the home river. Field research on big rivers involves a lot of driving, looking for physical vantage points from which to visually assess the nature of the river — elevated roadside cuttings, or a nearby hill. Where they exist, old logging skid sites can provide some of the best river views, or get together with a mate and hire a plane. It will save years of footwork!

One of the key frustrations associated with bigger rivers is that, while they may well provide a greater volume of productive water, there will also be significant areas of unproductive water to avoid. The art of recognising high percentage water and dismissing low percentage water is one of the greatest skills in productive flyfishing and particularly relevant in any approach to bigger water.

On bigger rivers, often there are combinations of several "productive parcels" in one area and a target hot spot is where the number of productive parcels is maximised and the distance between them minimised. These are worth searching for and on rivers with well-defined courses, prize water may remain relatively stable from year to year. On many of our big braided rivers, however, the quest for productive water generally begins

Lake Hawea's edges support many cruising fish on regular beats
[PHOTO: DAVID HALLETT]

A tight line and "walking the dog" [PHOTO: ROSS MILLICHAMP]

Hooked up in the weed beds of Waikaremoana [PHOTO: DAVID HALLETT]

Extraordinary stealth is a requisite to even get close to south Waikato spring creek trout [PHOTO: DAVID HALLETT]

A prime winter run Tongariro rainbow
[PHOTO: BOB SOUTH]

This Karamea brown fell to a small black gnat
[PHOTO: KRIS SHEPHERD]

Drift fishing the south Westland lakes can be highly rewarding [PHOTO: TONY ENTWISTLE]

Mastering a difficult trout [PHOTO: ZANE MIRFIN]

again each season.

As with other angling, consideration of the habits of your quarry is essential and the key is to concentrate your angling on the prime water that gives the trout what it needs. If you are trying to catch feeding trout (most of the time), then sort out the prime feeding areas. If you are trying to tempt trout that are not feeding (e.g. on a spawning run), sort out the prime sheltering lies. Fishing the right water will always provide a head start on those who may have impressive mechanical skills, but don't take the time to choose good water.

Arguably, anglers don't fish a river, but simply approach it to fish different water types. That's why reading water is the most elemental skill. River fishing, regardless of the size, is a combination of fishing the different "parcels" of water comprised of runs, pools, riffles, pocket water, backwaters, flats, edges, eyes, and tailouts. Being able to identify water types and recognise their opportunities refines your approach and narrows the choice of techniques. This information needs to be further modified by considerations of the time of year and the fundamentals of water temperature, clarity, and flow. Much of the daunting aspect of big rivers is more about working out the suitable water to fish, rather than the angling technique to be employed. However, unless you are the lucky recipient of a hot tip, this can only be achieved by walking and fishing them.

Regardless of the size of a river, trout are very much "creatures of the margins". As American author John Gierach eloquently puts it in *Trout Bum* (1986): "They operate at the edges of things: fast and slow currents, deep and shallow water, air and stream, light and darkness, and the angler who understands that is well on his way to knowing what he is doing."

For the walk and wade fly angler, the most obvious limitation to water that can be fished is casting distance. Pragmatically, when the water exceeds wading depth, anything beyond casting distance is purely of aesthetic value. However, it is a misconception (probably born from the limitations of flycasting distance) that on the biggest rivers trout avoid the central areas because of the weight and depth of the water and stick only to areas close to the structure of the banks. Aerial and drift surveys by Otago Fish & Game on the Clutha River (New Zealand's largest mean flow) reveal that trout are quite evenly spread across most of the river, favouring, if anything, the centre of the river more during the daytime. Surface flow characteristics do not represent a fish's immediate holding environment. River trout in New Zealand generally inhabit moderate water velocities (0.2–0.5 metres per second) with recent research (Hayes) suggesting that brown trout prefer "on the nose" velocity limits of between 0.2–0.3 metres per second, but will move briefly to feed in water column velocities of 0.3–0.5 metres per second. These velocity ranges are safely achieved among the bottom structure of most of our boulder strewn, freestone rivers, regardless of size.

The physiology of brown and rainbow trout is quite different. Rainbows are adapted to spending more time in the water column than browns and accordingly are better able to ultilise faster water velocities. This is reflected in the observed difference in distribution of rainbows and browns across a river, with larger resident browns particularly frequenting the shallower, quieter margins of a river, while rainbows stick to the deeper, faster water further out.

Very deep holes and deep water generally (over 4–5m) looks very attractive to new chums, but it is what I regard as 1% water. In reality, it presents serious practical problems for any fly angler to catch fish. While these areas may provide "shelter water" for some trout, they are unlikely to support much algal growth (due to the lack of light to promote photosynthesis) and, therefore, don't hold the grazing invertebrates that make up most of our trout's diet.

Practically, especially where surface water velocities far exceed trout holding velocities, drag also makes it difficult for flies to sink deep enough or drift naturally in this water, regardless of how heavily nymphs are weighted.

While modern sink tip and sinking line technology offers some options, this isn't top "feeding water". Unless trout are visible cruising on the top (generally only in slow currents) and present obvious opportunities for dry fly, emerger, or lighter weighted nymph tactics, I suggest walking on by. It is barely worth 1% of angling effort, although I see huge amounts more time wasted on it.

There is a temptation with big rivers to take a more brutal approach than on small streams. But while there may be a bit more latitude in approaching the water, care still needs to be taken not to unnecessarily scare the fish. Any approach to a potential fishing area should be conducted quietly and conservatively, because the same rule applies — "spook one fish, maybe spook the lot". On big water that is likely to equate to a lot more fish, with the downside that, as mentioned earlier, it is probably going to be quite a hike to the next parcel of productive water.

It is generally harder to spot fish on big rivers, particularly on windy or overcast days because of the bigger expanses of water and the frequent lack of a dark background. When it isn't possible to spot easily, focus on areas that have a backdrop of trees or high banks. The high banks are also useful for spotting with the advantage of height, which also eliminates glare. Ultimately, however, to become a consistently successful fisher of big waters, an angler will require the development and refinement of good blind (imaginative) fishing techniques. When stalking, spotting, and casting to sighted trout it often begs the question: Did you simply spot the fish, or did your eyes confirm what you expected to see? Mostly I suspect it is the latter, in which case intelligent blind fishing is a lot less about chuck and chance and more about testing an angler's suspicions and aspirations. The better an angler gets at reading water, the more imagination can be applied and more success results. It is perhaps worth noting that the most successful blind fishermen I know are, without exception, also the best trout spotters. Both approaches to fishing any water are complimentary, especially on big rivers.

The time of year significantly influences what types of "water parcel" to focus on. Early season is the toughest time to successfully fish big rivers, with angling opportunity limited by high water levels, cold water temperatures, and difficult wading. Fish will tend to hold in slightly deeper water, so it is best to concentrate on areas of slower flows in the established holding water, such as mid-depth pools and big runs. The best places are where the river meanders and flows into features, such as bedrock cliffs and high banks, or along areas of riverbank stabilisation, with extended areas of willows or rip-rap. Where the water depth is generally less than two metres (most river trout are taken from less than 2m), standard heavy weighted nymphing techniques, using floating lines, will probably be most productive. However, where the water is deeper, or coloured, or if temperatures are cold (below 7°C), time spent fishing streamer flies, using sinking line technology (from sink tips through to deepwater express shooting heads), is also worthwhile. Big water presents the opportunity to use a much wider variety of techniques than is typical of small streams, especially downstream techniques. Sinking line techniques, using streamers and nymphs, can be effective on big waters throughout the season and more anglers should use them, especially when trout are clearly not evident in more easily spotted shallow water. Development of a range of downstream techniques will also help extend an angler's time on big water, especially when confronted with strong afternoon headwinds typical of most exposed big valley systems, which severely handicap standard upstream dead drift techniques.

Most anglers would also do better using heavier weight rods (#7 to #8) during the early part of the season to better cope with winds and heavy nymphs.

Bigger rivers come into their own as the season progresses for a number of reasons and by mid-summer can become the hot spots in many areas. As river flows drop and water temperatures climb, fish become more active for longer periods and start spreading around. Areas of pocket water, most usually associated with the narrowing or gorging of a riverbed, will now be worthy of interest and expect brown trout at least to move to shallower water (0.4–1.5m). Floating lines, fished using heavy and medium weighted nymphs, will be productive. Look for the start of good dry fly action too, especially during the coloburiscus hatches characteristic of most New Zealand rivers from mid-November through to mid-late-December.

By January, the strong equinox winds that can plague the exposed valleys of large rivers will have started to ease and, if an angler is lucky, they won't become too much of a casting hazard until mid-late afternoon.

During the height of summer and early autumn when river flows drop to their lowest, more fishable water is exposed and many big rivers lose some of their intimidation factor. As they become more benevolent and easier to get around on, big rivers have real appeal, especially as fishing on small streams often deteriorates as their trout populations become stressed from low flows and warm water.

When water temperatures rise, focus on the prime feeding areas created by shallow riffles (sexy water). These are associated with ledges and dropoffs at the heads of pools and adjacent to deep runs and will hold good concentrations of active trout. Areas of a river that favour riffle development generally occur in association with a widening of the riverbed.

Another largely overlooked "productive parcel", which frequently presents itself to the walk and wade angler when big rivers drop to their lowest levels, is found in any extensive areas of flat water that were unwadeable earlier in the season due to water depth and force of current. These large areas of flats are characterised by relatively even water depth and laminar surface flow and, in brown trout territory at least, are often favoured by good numbers of small (<0.5kg) to mid-sized fish (up to 1.5–2.0 kg). The smallest fish will tend to congregate in small pods and are usually impossible to approach, but the better fish will spread themselves and hold in association with any slightly larger stones or depressions in the substrate that create a break in the bottom current velocity. Here the best approach is to work slowly and quietly upstream, zigzagging across the water as far as safe wading allows searching for individual fish. Because these areas require stalking and spotting, success tends to be limited to calm, bright, sunny days with a high sun angle from behind and to areas with a backdrop of trees to facilitate spotting the fish. The smooth water characteristics created by the laminar surface flow requires fine 5x-6x tippets (fluorocarbon provides significant benefits in this situation) and small #16 to #20 flies, with my preference being small bead caddis nymphs or parachute dries. The prospects of stalking this sort of previously unfished water in high summer is always a tantalising prospect. So look for these areas during any early season excursions, making mental notes of potential prospects if the water level ever drops sufficiently. Good flats will often provide several hours of fishing in a relatively short distance for the careful and patient angler.

January to February is cicada time throughout most New Zealand regions and, where they exist, it is a special time of excitement and opportunity on big water, with many otherwise seemingly untouchable trout appearing. Fish will position adjacent to prominent current lines and it pays to work those big dries along any tree-lined runs, or areas flanked with rip-rap and grassed banks. Often good feeding lines lie on the far side of the current from the angler and it is not possible to change banks to attack rising fish in the conventional manner. The problem with trying to attack any fish from a downstream position across a current is that there will be almost instant drag on the fly. An excellent technique in these circumstances (where it is possible to wade into a position upstream of the drift line and cast the necessary distance across the river) is to cast the cicada slightly downstream on an angle (30–45 degrees), incorporating an up-stream reach and then start walking the fly downstream.

It is essentially the same technique employed from a drift boat, without the obvious advantages of a secure floatation device...so be wary of any sudden changes in depth! With the inclusion of some slack line and regular mending, it is possible to achieve regular floats of 20 metres or more before having to re-cast. The bonus is picking off some trout that are usually safe on the far side of the current.

At the other extreme of summer dry fly fishing, big water also frequently provides wonderful opportunities for early morning spinner falls, when trout feed profusely on the fallen bounty in the slower waters of any extensive flats and broad tailouts. These trout seldom hold a position and actively range across wide areas, hoovering the small, spent mayflies off the surface. It is not uncommon to see a dozen or more trout on the surface at the same time, but success can be elusive. Small low profile dries, such as a Parachute Adams, or specialist spinner patterns in sizes #14 to #20 are usually effective. The secret, though, is to target an individual fish, waiting until it rises before immediately dropping the dry fly centimetres directly ahead of its feeding path. Long drifts are seldom desirable, because before your fly reaches the rising position the fish is likely to have moved several metres away again on another tack. Water that often appears smooth also can be notoriously difficult to maintain a drag-free drift for any distance. When trout come up on a spinner fall, they are seldom up for more than an hour (two at the most) and often much less, so casting becomes a precision game, if the angler is to maximise the opportunity.

A common problem on big open waters from early January to early March, especially on the fine, clear, sunny days most preferable for fishing big waters, is for water temperatures to quickly climb out of the productive fish catching range (11–17°C). When the temperature climbs to 19°C (which is not uncommon on big braided riverbeds like Marlborough's Wairau River between 1.30pm to 3.30pm), trout will very quickly go off the feed until the water temperature starts to drop again. This means successful angling is most likely early morning or late evening.

Big rivers support huge caddis populations and prolific evening hatches are often a feature. This is a time when trout, which have been laying low under the shelter of the deeper water in the centre of large rivers, move into the shallower margins to chase hatching caddis. Once again, big water lends itself to downstream techniques and traditional down-and-across small wet fly (soft hackle) techniques can prove very effective in these circumstances, especially on trout rising in the more boisterous water, where it is not possible to keep track of a dead-drifted dry fly. Small wet flies fished down-and-across can also be effective in similar water during daytime caddis and mayfly hatches and are worth attempting.

Because of their size and because regular success will require improved blind fishing techniques, big waters start to place a premium on casting skills. I often hear the obviously self-limiting excuse that: "I catch all my fish within 10 metres anyway, so I don't have to cast a long way." But undoubtedly, improving your ability to handle a longer line simply opens up more angling opportunities on big rivers. If you struggle to cast a line longer than 10–15m, then swallow your pride and get tuition…you will be amazed at the progress within only a couple of lessons.

There is a point where rivers, particularly in their lower regions, become so big that bank fishing and wading opportunities become limited. Generally, these areas become the preserve of livebait anglers or spin fishermen, but the fly angler, who can sort out a point and work a streamer fly down the current line and along the banks, still has an opportunity, especially early and late in the season when a few sea-run trout are present. As rivers grow in size, the use of a boat significantly expands opportunities and is ideal where access is difficult, or few bank or wade fishing opportunities exist. Over time, boats will play a bigger part in our fishing scene, especially if access rights to the banks of our rivers continue to be eroded.

Success on big water is fundamentally about approach, not simply mechanics. Ultimately, successfully flyfishing big rivers depends as much on attitude as the depth of angling skills, and managing and overcoming the psychological intimidation is the priority.

An old timer once put it to me that when approaching a big river "just think of it as two small rivers…one up either side". While it has proved a bit of a simplification, his advice certainly encouraged me to look at big water differently and gave me a focus. What this old chap was really suggesting was to minimise the uncertainty of big water by breaking the river up into familiar "parcels" and then concentrating on what was in front of me. This is after all, the simple essence of flyfishing any water.

Muddy Waters

BY ZANE MIRFIN

The rain continued to thump down on the iron roof of our backcountry "Hilton" while we lay in our sleeping bags. It had poured all night and I was dreading getting up to look at the state of the river.

Daylight came and our worst fears were confirmed, as the river was again a brown swollen torrent. This was our fourth day in a row in similar conditions. A nasty series of fronts had swept out of the Tasman Sea and caught weather forecasters napping and had seriously impacted on this particular guiding trip.

Fortunately my pair of Australian anglers were fun, upbeat, and prepared to do what it took to be successful. Each day we would wait for the river to drop slightly and then race out for a few hours of fishing before it began to rise again. Our last day, unplanned because the chopper could not negotiate the mountains to reach us the afternoon before, was a bonus because it later turned out that virtually everywhere else in the South Island had totally blown out. In late evening, sitting beside the fire supplementing our dwindling rations with fresh trout and our last bottle of red wine, the whine of the helicopter turbines signaled the end of another successful adventure.

Muddy waters can drive any sane angler to drink. Virtually all of us would much rather fish in fine weather with clear, pristine water. However, the reality is that without rain and flood events we would not have the great fishing resources that we do in New Zealand. The cycles of nature have always ruled the hunting and fishing activities of man and will always continue to do so. Truly successful anglers have the ability to adapt to any conditions by understanding the cycles of nature and fishing smart within the opportunities available. It is always disappointing when you plan fishing holidays and your arrival at your chosen location coincides with torrential rainfall and floods of biblical proportions. But all is not lost and good anglers can often make the best of a bad situation.

As a fulltime guide with almost two decades of experience, I have seen my fair share of crappy conditions. Customers have booked fishing days and are expecting to catch fish and I need the work to feed my family — therefore we go fishing regardless of the conditions. One thing I have learned over the years is that trout have to feed to survive and, by understanding the nature of the beast, it is often possible to have great fishing where others fear to tread. Usually you will have whole river systems to yourself in times of bad weather and high flows.

A little thought, innovation, and persistence will put some big fish in the net for you while most other people are sitting at home making excuses.

To enjoy fishing in adverse conditions you need to have the right equipment. If you are going to enjoy yourself when conditions are grim, then you need to invest in the equipment that will keep you warm, dry, and able to brave any environmental conditions that occur. When you go fishing you should always take good rain gear and waders are always an excellent choice, if you intend standing around in bad weather. Thermal clothing can also assist comfort levels during such times.

Standard flyfishing equipment is fine for fishing in rising or falling rivers and lakes. Along with floating lines, intermediate and sink tip lines, including poly leaders, can all be useful in getting your flies down to where the fish can see them. Use shorter leaders to assist casting efficiency and reduce tangles, as well as heavier tippets to salvage flies from snags and to enable trout to be "horsed" out of tight locations and heavy flows. Use larger and brighter flies than normal. If the fish are feeding, they will be hungry and they can only eat what they can see. Trout will eat very large flies, both nymphs and streamers, in times of high flow.

Spinning outfits are always useful in high flow situations and allow anglers to cover a lot of water with minimal effort. They are a great way for inexperienced or junior anglers to catch vulnerable trout in otherwise adverse conditions. My favourite lures are floating Rapalas that can attract trout like metal to a magnet when nothing else will work. Sometimes heavy chunky lures, such as a 14gram Toby, are the way to go. Such lures can get deeper in the water column and be nearer to the bottom where the trout will be lurking. Expect to sacrifice plenty of hardware to the fishing gods when fishing murky water though!

Safety is paramount when fishing in less than ideal conditions. Take no chances when near rising rivers, as drowning is a very real possibility. Always make sure you are on the right side of the river when rain begins and that you know where alternative exit points are should you get caught out. Many times during my guiding career, we have been caught out. Once we abandoned my truck on one side of a ford as we ran for cover when rivers rose dramatically. Another time we sat most of a day in one spot, trapped by rising waters, hoping the chopper would get back to us. Another day saw us climbing out of a massive gorge as an unexpected "wall of water" took us by surprise. On another trip, I spent a freezing cold night out without any gear, trapped opposite the hut, while my companions enjoyed a warm but worried night. Nowadays I like to carry a small foil emergency blanket in case of another unexpected night out, or injury. Hypothermia is a killer and, if you are away from your vehicle, you should be prepared. I consider myself fortunate to have experienced dozens of such adventures, but as I grow older and wiser and my body begins to creak and groan I know that taking risks is stupid. Know when to quit and wait patiently for the conditions to improve. If in doubt, don't do it!

Fish will still feed on a rising river, but the window of

opportunity is small, especially if the water level and clarity are deteriorating quickly. Brown trout will move toward the edges, in surprisingly calm water, and can be targeted by either sight fishing or casting blind to likely locations.

As a river blows out and goes from milky coloured to raging brown floodwater, it is time to quit and head for cover. Often another stream in another catchment may be a good bet, as rain conditions may be different or the stream conditions more resilient to bad weather. Fortunately in New Zealand, we have a multitude of rivers and another catchment may only be a short drive away. Streams draining native bush often rise more slowly and clear faster than highly modified lowland pasture streams, for example. Experience is important here with some clever thinking and willingness to drive around often resulting in some excellent discoveries that may be useful another time. In heavy flow periods, spring creeks, flooded lake edges, clear stream confluences, backwaters, lake inlets and outlets all offer hope to enthusiastic anglers.

In eastern South Island areas, alluvial rivers will often flow discoloured and milky for weeks on end due to the influence of the mighty nor'wester. Trout can be caught in surprisingly milky water, but it is best if the water is turning a green or blue tinge to indicate a clearing phase. Often small streams and springs, where clear water flows from the gravel, will prove to be a magnet for trout in such rivers. West Coast rivers will often flow dark tannin colour once the initial sediment load has been discharged and can offer good fishing, despite high flows and difficult access.

The best phase to fish murky water is when the water is clearing and the level falling. In some catchments, particularly on the South Island's West Coast and Fiordland, rivers can rise and fall in the space of a few short hours. Knowing the hydrological specifications of your local rivers can sometimes see you fishing within hours of heavy rainfall. Many river catchments now have automated data flow records accessible via regional council websites. Such websites can save a lot of driving and also show whether the water trend is rising or falling. For example in one gorgy river I fish, I know if the level is above seven cumecs, it is unwadeable and it is better to fish a more accessible location. Often it is possible to watch weather forecasts and plan to take a morning off fishing, sleep in, or have a nice breakfast out and let the front pass through. Once the front has passed, the weather will clear, the barometric pressure will rise, and even though the river may not be dropping much, the fish will begin to feed.

When fishing in adverse conditions, it is imperative to not try to fish everywhere in a river. Be selective and only fish the most likely places. Many New Zealand trout streams have limited fish stocks, so only fish the obvious pools and runs and don't be deceived by the attractiveness of other areas through increased water flow. Trout will seek clear water and will also avoid strong mid-current positions. Rainbows will still tend to station themselves in deeper and faster sections than browns, but it is imperative to get your flies near the bottom structure, which trout will gravitate toward.

High, discoloured water can actually be turned to advantage, as big trophy trout are often most vulnerable at this time.

Because they need to feed almost constantly, they often come close to shore to escape the current and feed in the clearer and more sheltered edge locations. Edges, grass banks, side channels, backwaters, and rocky structures are all likely places to investigate.

I now fish much browner water than before my American fishing experiences. When I first flew into Aspen, Colorado, I looked at the swollen Roaring Fork River from the plane with dismay. When I commented to the boss about the river, I was told that it was prime and that the catching was great. My first day fishing the snowmelt-fed river, I nymphed along the edges "brown trout style" and took 80 sassy rainbows. To say I was impressed was an understatement, especially after the chocolate milkshake water and pounding flows. At the fly shop, I was later taught the "bozo rig", which consisted of a six or eight foot leader, six adhesive backed strike indicators placed on the butt section, several inches apart. On the terminal end, double #6–8 Prince nymphs were attached to 0–2x, and just above them lead weight in the form of lead strips and large removable split shot was added in liberal doses. This rig was impossible to cast conventionally, but was lobbed up and across stream and was perfect to teach beginner tourist anglers how to flyfish. The trick was to keep adding weight until you caught fish, the rationale being that, if they don't eat it, they wear it. It was an incredibly effective method with rainbows, browns, and whitefish gobbling the big flies with abandon. On occasion, a large spawning sucker would be foul-hooked and the angler would see a large metre long golden flank rolling underwater. Some guides would start yelling, "big brown, big brown", knowing that landing such a foul-hooked sucker was impossible in such heavy flows and also hoping that the angler would go away thinking they had lost the trophy of a lifetime and re-book for the following year!

Upstream and across stream nymphing is probably the most common and most successful fishing method in high murky flows, but can have disadvantages, especially if strong downstream winds or heavy rainfall are encountered. Heavy rainfall will sink indicators and make visual detection of takes difficult and also the high degree of concentration required becomes tiring. Wind can make fishing a dangerous occupation, as weighted flies go everywhere and the effort of fighting the wind seriously reduces fishing enjoyment.

Down and across fishing, using either a pair of large nymphs, rubber leg flies, or streamers, often works well because the fish hook themselves. Throwing a short leader, especially on a sink-tip line, is far easier and the angler can also cover more water in a more relaxing manner. Spin fishing has the advantage of being a no-brainer in relation to casting effort, can cover large distances of water very effectively, and can also be a more pleasant method of tackling larger water. I enjoy throwing a spinner occasionally and make no apology for resorting to this most effective method whenever it is required. Whatever method you fish in high flows, you should be getting snags or touching bottom regularly because this is where the fish will be if you cannot see them on the edges.

Whatever fishing methods you choose, be optimistic and

persevere, for with experience and dedication you will be surprised at what treasures you can pull out of water that originally appeared unfishable. Marvel at the wonders of the environment and the power of nature as you wait for that next eight pounder to start tugging on your line.

During the annual Nelson One Fly Competition in March 2002, which coincided with the worst river conditions encountered by contestants in the 11 years the competition has been running, guide Dave Eccleston was quoted as saying that the "water was too thick to drink and too thin to plough". The important thing to note here, however, is that many trout were caught despite the conditions.

Muddy waters are both a blessing and a curse. To fish or not to fish — that is always the question and always up to the motivation of the individual angler. Try your luck in murky flows sometime. You may be pleasantly surprised.

Hard at it in ideal pocket water [PHOTO: DAVID HALLETT]

A saucy sight for any angler [PHOTO: DAVID HALLETT]

An imminent release [PHOTO: DAVID HALLETT]

Slurping down a natural [PHOTO: DAVID HALLETT]

A real pig of a brown [PHOTO: LES HILL]

Concentration is integral to success [PHOTO: LES HILL]

A classic cast on the Rangitikei River [PHOTO: BOB SOUTH]

Feed time on the Wangapeka [PHOTO: DAVID HALLETT]
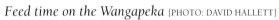

Fishing Sexy Water

BY TONY ENTWISTLE

Fishing riffles is anything but chuck and chance. To be consistently successful you must use your eyes... it's that "whole visual thing" — identifying the water, the lies, presentation, and drift. Of course, you need to wade well, cast a lot more, exercise a consistently high degree of line control, but mostly, you require imagination. Get it right and plenty of fish will be caught from comparatively small amounts of water.

Riffles are the shallow water in a river, ranging from centimetres to about 1.2 metres, where the energy flow is dissipated by collision with the substrate and is manifested as irregular, turbulent, and choppy surface water. As noted American angling author Dave Whitlock puts it, riffles are "...noisy, exciting, bright areas that appear to dance in the sunlight".

Trout need shelter, abundant accessible food, and suitable water temperatures. Areas where these are found are known as "prime lies". New Zealand streams and rivers have abundant trout invertebrate insects of a large average size. Much of the time trout can fill their stomachs quickly if they find a place where food is concentrated, then they retreat to a location to metabolise the food. How quickly a fish comes back on the feed depends on how quickly it metabolises that food. When water temperatures are cold, this may happen only once a day, but when temperatures are in the optimum range (11–17°C), it happens more often. Trout are aided in feeding by the clarity of many of our waterways. Once in a feeding position, they establish a foraging area and generally the clearer the water, the larger the trout's foraging area. On this basis, what makes riffles stack up as suitable trout habitat?

Gary Borger in his book, *Nymphing A Basic Book* (1979), provides the following description: "The rubble bottom provides the greatest possible number of niches for the trout and his food organisms, and the moving water brings a continuous flood of oxygen and nutrients into the area. Fish will feel very secure under the choppy surface, and if the water is at least a couple of feet deep, the entire riffle should he considered a prime lie... Shallow riffles are feeding lies. Fish move into these places during dawn, dusk, and at night."

Whitlock writes in his *Guide to Aquatic Trout Foods:* "A riffle provides the best opportunity for water to purify itself by filtration. It expels excess gases such as the carbon dioxide produced by the breakdown of plant and animal waste. Water also accepts the important oxygen and other gases from the air in a riffle. Such hypercirculation greatly encourages the establishment of the largest colonies... of trout foods."

Trout feed on the margins, wherever current lines tend to concentrate and transport food. They lie in a reasonably sheltered, "neutral" flow situation alongside a current line and move in and out of that zone to pick up food. These "forage zones" are often quite small and specific — dependent upon water speed, visibility, food size and quantity, and water temperature. Riffles create a multitude of small, but highly productive forage zones that often sustain feeding lies for large numbers of trout at any one time. This is particularly so for browns.

My experience suggests riffles that run from 25–80cm deep are most productive, as they are the most easily waded and fished. They are more than simply a break between the deep water of a pool and shallow water of a rapid (a shelf) and will feature large, deep holding water (runs or pools) downstream. Typically that holding water will feature good sheltering areas, such as deep water running against a cliff or bank, maybe areas of large boulders/rocks, or deep long runs flanked by undercut banks or willow trees.

Riffles are a feature of big, broad freestone rivers where the substrate has been graded to range from gravel to rocks of around 30cm in diameter. However, streams of all sizes have riffles of various dimensions and importance, even spring creeks, and different angling techniques will have varying degrees of relevance on most rivers and streams.

The best riffles are often found on the big water of New Zealand's larger low country rivers, such as the Buller, Wairau, and Motueka. Many anglers are intimidated by large streams, but as an oldtimer once encouraged me: "Just think of a big river as two small rivers... one up either side!"

The beauty of riffles is that they are usually wadeable and even on big rivers they can extend quite a long way across, creating a huge area of productive water to prospect.

Riffle fishing improves as river levels drop to median or lower flows and results depend to a large degree on a river's temperature regime. On low country braided streams, riffles become most productive with temperatures between 13–17°C. Above 19°C, trout quickly lose interest in feeding and will only feed for brief periods before moving back into cooler depths of sheltering water below. However, when water temperatures reach this upper level, riffles are the best place to have a chance of successful angling as fish seek out the most oxygenated water and higher insect count.

Riffle fishing is a summer to late season phenomenon, starting as early as late November/early December, peaking in February, and sometimes carrying on into mid-April in warmer seasons.

However, productive riffle fishing can occur any time, if circumstances are right. Low rivers and extended periods of fine, warm weather have become an increasing phenomenon in September/October in recent years. Riffles can also become instantly hot places to fish on a rising river just prior to a fresh at any time of year.

If late daytime temperatures exceed 19°C, riffle fishing is best early morning when water temperatures are coolest.

When rivers drop to their lowest mid-summer flows, trout

often concentrate in large numbers in riffles to take advantage of better oxygenation and food supplies. Trout are difficult, if not impossible; to spot in riffles and by the simple process of deduction, if they aren't visible in the easy to see water, start fishing the water you can't see as clearly. Trout are normally there somewhere — when water temperatures are low and river levels high, they will generally be in deeper runs, but as levels drop and temperatures rise, the riffles produce.

It's possible to spot trout in riffles, even without sunshine, particularly when the riffle has a dark backdrop. During bright sunshine, an angler may pick the trout's shadows, or the dark moss green or blue grey silhouettes of their backs by wading up from behind. I like to get out into the river as far as I can below the water I want to fish and visualise the various current lanes coming towards me. With a bit of imagination the water starts to look like a bit of ragged graph paper with a multitude of flow lines spreading and merging. These are principal lines I will drift my flies along.

Within a riffle there are other clues as to where the trout will lie. Any darkening of water colour tends to indicate an increase in the depth of the riffle at that point. These are prime lies and are also generally evidenced by what experienced anglers call slicks. Slicks often have a characteristic V shape. Those created by a single obstruction (like a rock) will appear as an inverted V (opening towards the angler), while slicks created by a shelf or ledge appear as a V opening away from the angler and are generally much bigger than ones created by an object. Larger slicks are where many trout often feed in close proximity and may well have a series of "small object" slicks contained within them, especially in their shallower upper section.

Generally, the most productive daytime riffle fishing technique is nymphing. Given the high density of aquatic insects resident in good fishing riffles, there are always plenty of nymphs being dislodged by the turbulent water in addition to the natural downstream insect drift. New chums should start by fishing only one nymph, but graduate as quickly as possible to two. Using two flies more than doubles your success rate.

I rig my nymphs several ways, depending on the size and weight of the flies and the depth and speed of the water. Because I am mostly trying to set up a drag-free drift, which relies on the creation of some slack line, I use an indicator, generally of pale neutral colours. They are a little more difficult to see, but are clearly less visible to trout and less likely to scare them. Set the indicator very close to the fly, depending on current speed, water depth, and fly weight — usually not more than one metre above the top fly… or the only fly if you are using a single nymph. I often reduce this distance to around 70cm in fast shallow riffles such as are found in many parts of the mid to lower Buller, just to be onto the strike quickly enough. Experimentation is the key to learning what depth is best. As a rule, shorter is better — approximately two times the water depth you are fishing.

Because of the shallow water in riffles, the indicator doesn't always dive each take. Quite commonly, it simply hesitates briefly and many anglers won't read this as a take. Believe what your indicator is telling you and strike at all small hesitations. Many will be fish!

Leaders do not have to be long, around 3.54m for most situations. Standard floating line rigs are suitable. Line weights #5 or #6 are best in most waters. Modest to lightly weighted flies work best as water depths are shallow.

Getting into the water and fishing directly upstream into riffles is normally the best approach, hence the need to be a reasonable wader. It is not often possible to fish for any extended period directly upstream, due to the broken nature of the water and the varying current lines. I employ a zig-zag wading pattern as I move into a riffle, but there's still the need to cast across current lines a lot of the time. As a riffle curves, this becomes increasingly necessary. Try not to cast too far, or across too many different current lanes. The broken water and noisy nature of riffles means you can position yourself much closer to feeding lies than in most other types of water (pocket water excepted). Effective casts are little more than 5–8m. Drag becomes an instant problem when laying line across a faster flow.

Deft mending preserves a drag-free drift for as long as possible, which in many cases may only be achievable for distances of 1–3m. However, short drifts are not a problem, given the broken nature of the water, the relatively short distance and time the trout has to sight food and make quick decisions to take any fly. Achieving depth in fast riffles deeper than 40cm, without creating bulky flies, is important. Beadheads have greatly helped success rates in this type water.

To create a drag-free drift in a curving or crosscurrent riffle, two principal elements need to be included in the presentation cast and drift. The first is a reach cast. For righthanders, it's much easier to establish a good drift, fishing into a left-to-right flowing riffle. Being able to reach cast in right-to-left flowing riffles is essential for righthanders. The second element is the ability to sustain a series of short, quick rotational mends. This is achieved by holding the rod high, with an extended casting arm, and executing the mends with a continuous flicking of the rod tip, (up, left, right, up, left, right, and so on). I call this the "dancing-line technique", as the line is in a continuous and fluid motion, preventing the body of the line from becoming trapped in any faster or slower flow between the angler and the desired drift lane, for as long as possible. Because we are only laying out a short cast, big slow aerial mends that lift and relay the belly of the line will do nothing to minimise drag.

Never overlook the very whitest water at the upper limit of a riffle, where the water breaks over a ledge. This highly aerated water is top holding water, especially during the height of summer, so always drift your fly in above this white water by at least a metre or two. Takes will be short and hard to pick up, so strike at any hesitation of the indicator.

An alternative nymphing technique in riffles interspersed with runs or pockets deeper than 0.8m involves short casts and a tight line, where the angler is essentially maintaining direct contact with the fly and feeling for the weight of the trout as it takes the fly. This form of short line nymphing is a practised and deadly touch for those who master it. European anglers are very skilful with this technique and many beadhead nymph patterns were developed for it. Stand directly across from the lie and hold the rod high, using a series of small rotational tip mends to minimise drag on the line and fly, all the time maintaining tension enough between the rod tip and the fly to be able to feel any takes. An indicator is seldom used and leader length is no more than 3m. Two flies are effective.

When trout are rising, especially to caddis flies, a dry fly can greatly simplify fishing some riffles. The best all-round riffle dry fly has to be the Elk Hair (Troth's) Caddis, because of its floatability and visibility. There are many variations, including a range of high floating CDC caddis patterns. My next favourite riffle dry is the Parachute Adams. Its low profile and good visibility make it successful in all but the most boisterous riffles.

Throughout January and February, fishing various large cicada patterns is often the easiest and most successful approach to riffles, producing some spectacular hits.

Occasionally combine a dry fly with a nymph dropper. This technique works in the broadest, more even flowing and gentler riffles where there are fewer complications with drag. However, I prefer to specialise when fishing riffles, using either the two nymph combo or the dry fly by itself, as these reduce difficulties created by varying water flows at different depths (even in quite shallow water), which are exacerbated when the dry/nymph combo is attempted.

Not all riffle fishing needs to be undertaken on the dead-drift principle. Riffles often create opportunities to fish downstream. Trout are much more forgiving of angler scent in low country streams and in many rivers, like the Motueka and Pelorus, it is possible to get close to the drift lanes, above feeding fish, especially when trout are actively rising to caddis or during a heavy mayfly hatch. This is when traditional down-and-across small wet fly techniques work particularly well.

Enter slightly above the riffle and work systematically downstream through it, casting across at about 45–60 degrees and allowing the fly/flies to sweep down and around, moving down a metre or so after every second cast. Watch for bulges and swirls of bigger fish that will not break the water in splashy rises characteristic of smaller trout. When fish are hitting hard I have had as many as 20 takes in under an hour from one riffle. Generally, I use two flies on this approach — either two small wet flies or soft hackles, or an Elk Hair Caddis on the top fly (bob-fly) and a small wet or soft hackle below. The Elk Hair Caddis is sometimes taken as a dry in the first few feet of the drift, before it starts to swing. Thereafter, it is hit as it sets up a wake across the surface. These are always spectacular takes as the fly is buried in a violent swirl.

Another direct downstream technique involves the use of a sunken line. Use either a Teeny T130 (#5, #6 rods), or T200 (#7 rod) sink tip line. These are easy to cast and sink rapidly. Leaders are short (1.5–2m max) and stout (min 2.8g). I favour two flies, usually using soft hackles (#12, #14 often with a gold beadhead) on the top dropper and small beadhead marabou streamers (#12) on the point. I have also had success using a single Green Stonefly Nymph #10.

My technique combines a mixture of down-and-across on the swing, with a slow walk downstream, stripping and twitching the fly as I move. If the trout don't take at the beginning of the swing, they tend to hit as the fly straightens out below. At this point of the drift, I start the fly "dancing" with a series of flicks with the rod tip and some short strips. Along an undercut bank or overhanging willows, I'll "slip" the line out again to allow the fly to sink back close to or under the obstruction and commence to dance and strip the fly again.

The takes are awesome...a solid smack will stop the line dead and will generally be followed by a screaming run and leap...so be ready to lose some line!

I've taken browns and rainbows with this "strip-and-twitch" technique, but it's particularly effective on rainbows and sea-run trout and is a handy backup when strong downstream winds (common most afternoons on open South Island braided riverbeds) make upstream, dead-drift style fishing difficult or impossible.

Landing fish in a wide ripple requires special skills not necessary when an angler can make the security of the bank. A good net is essential. As trout will generally end up below an angler's position, most will be landed against the flow of the river. While this may appear impossible in fast water at first, the secret is to use the river flow to help you. Swing the fish downstream, directly below you. In this position there will be an eddy set up from your body breaking the current. Trial and error will make netting easier in time. However, it's your call whether you want to stay and battle the fish out in the riffle or make the wade back to the bank to have a more secure landing option.

Release trout in a large riffle in the eddy of any largish rock. If nothing is available and you are out above the knee, release the fish into the eddy you create. Fish will frequently slide up against your boot for the minute or so it takes to recover before they swim away.

Neighbours From Hell

BY JOHN HAYES

My first attempt at understanding the social life of trout ended with a trip to hospital. My father was helping me to make a flow-through fish observation tank for studying social interactions between brown and rainbow trout fry — an idea I had dreamed up for part of my PhD thesis. Dad saw it as a good opportunity to try out his new power planer and with it he made a neat job of shortening his left index finger by about one centimetre. After the hospital visit, Dad's role in the fish tank construction business was confined to project supervisor. Before long, Mark I and Mark II observation tanks were up and running beside my study stream — the main spawning and nursery creek for trout in Lake Alexandrina in the middle of the Mackenzie Country of the South Island.

By the time I began my voyeurism into the social life of trout fry, I had a pretty good grounding in the theory, having read just about all the books and scientific papers on the subject in the Canterbury University library. But seeing the trout display their fascinating repertoire of social behaviours with my own eyes was much more interesting. They totally fascinated me. What I was learning was the sign language that trout use to lay claim to space in which to secure food in streams. Rather than scramble for their food, which they do so occasionally, trout, most of the time, adhere to a set of innate behavioural rules that result in a fairly orderly partitioning of available feeding territories in streams — although this process is by no means polite or equitable.

As soon as they emerge from the spawning gravels as free swimming fry, trout and salmon exhibit aggressive behaviour toward other fry. At first, when there is not much size disparity among them, the fry divide the available feeding space into a territorial mosaic — that is, they spread out over the streambed roughly equidistant from each other and with roughly the same size territories. As they grow, the fry diverge in size owing to differences in the quality of the feeding territories. Eventually they outgrow their territories and have to move to new spots in faster, deeper water to ensure that their food supply keeps pace with their increasing metabolic requirements.

Territory size is related to fish size, getting bigger as the fish grow. A rule of thumb is that the average diameter of the territory of drift-feeding trout is about seven times the length of the fish. The boundaries of the defended area have been found to roughly correspond to the foraging area. However, some fish at some times can defend much larger territories. I once saw a dominant yearling trout (15cm) defend an area as large as five metres in diameter in a small river. This fish was like a little Hitler. Whenever it spotted another yearling feeding within sight, even two or more metres downstream, it would chase the "intruder" round and round the pool until it dived for cover under a rock. Sometimes even that did not satisfy the despot's megalomania. It would seek out the cringing subordinate and the pursuit would begin again.

Not all trout rigidly adhere to territorial strategies. Those that don't are termed "floaters", and these move from place to place — possibly eventually taking up territories if they find free space. A component of most trout populations is on the move at any point in time. In that manner, trout opportunistically exploit space that becomes available as other fish vacate feeding territories either voluntarily or by accident as a result of predation or floods. This is also how trout populations extend their range.

There is also some flexibility in the type of social structures that trout, and juvenile salmon, establish. In riffles, where currents are faster, juvenile trout adhere pretty rigidly to territories, which they attempt to defend from all-comers. In pools, social hierarchies are more common. In these social hierarchies, the dominant fish gets the best spot and beats up any fish that tries to muscle in upstream. Other fish fit in downstream and all are subordinate to the dominant fish. The next most dominant fish takes the next best spot below the top fish and defends its position against fish below it in the pecking order downstream. Social hierarchies are more fluid than territories, with some jostling for position going on now and then, especially when food becomes temporarily abundant. Probably the reason why territories are not the norm in pools is because the deeper water makes it difficult for fish to exclusively defend space in three dimensions. The drifting food is also more spatially variable in pools, being more focussed by flow constriction upstream and then diluting downstream owing to settling onto the riverbed as the flow spreads out and slows down. So the best spot is near the head of the pool, at least in small rivers, and all fish want to be near it.

The best feeding locations are occupied by dominant fish. These are usually closest to the source of incoming drift, such as near the heads of pools (just mentioned) and runs, and often with refuge cover nearby. Dominance confers definite benefits to the individuals; they grow faster and can experience greater survival. Dominance is associated with larger body size, prior residence, and species, in that order. Temperature also has an influence on species dominance as we shall see later.

Aggression is highest among fish of similar size — and being slightly bigger gives trout a competitive edge over their rivals. The survival advantage of being biggest is so important that it drives evolutionary pressure for trout to lay large eggs. The larger the egg, the bigger will be the resulting fry and the better its survival prospects. Trout that differ substantially in size, such as fry and yearlings, tend not to engage in aggressive encounters. This is partly because they eat differently sized prey so have no need to compete. Also, fry generally try to keep out of the way of larger fish to avoid being eaten.

The sign language or visual displays, which trout and young

salmon use to impose their dominance or assert territorial rights, is fascinating and took scientists quite some time to decipher. It is not until you observe trout undisturbed underwater, for some length of time, that you get a glimpse of these behaviours. And it is more common to see interactions among fry than among adults because fry are often numerous and close together. For these reasons, it is rare for anglers to encounter adult trout interacting socially — and you have to know what to look for. I can recall a few occasions when the trout I was fishing to became preoccupied with an interloper in its feeding territory. Sometimes you simply see the intruder chased off, but every now and then something more bizarre occurs. The two trout begin swimming stiffly side-by-side and then perhaps one will rout the other. In the meantime, the angler is left puzzled on the bank and frustrated that the trout have lost interest in the fly as a result of their preoccupation with the border dispute. This stiff side-by-side swimming behaviour is termed a "lateral display" by fish behaviourists. It is one of the more common social interactions among fry and is a relatively low level aggressive display. In the full blown form, the fish arch their bodies — head and tail upward — and flare their pectoral and pelvic fins down and their dorsal fin upward. When they get a little more agitated, they swim with exaggerated body undulations — a behaviour quaintly termed "wig wag" display. Another behaviour which ratchets up the seriousness of the aggressive interaction is the frontal display. The fish charges an intruder, flaring its pectoral fins down, opening its mouth, dropping its lower jaw, and flaring its gills. If this fails to drive off the intruder, then the gloves come off and the fish resort to chasing and nipping. A few nips can escalate to an all-out brawl, with the opponents slamming into one another, often knocking off scales. When young trout are all trying to establish territories, a lot of aggressive encounters can ensue. They argue and scrap: neighbours from hell.

The consistent losers of aggressive interactions end up displaying their low social status through behaviours and colourations that appear designed to reduce their conspicuousness to other fish. Subordinate fish skulk away from other fish, often hiding on the streambed under rocks and other cover, holding their dorsal fin down and other fins close to their sides. They lose their vibrant colours and, in juvenile fish, the boldness of their parr marks. Parr marks are a series of dark vertical ovals along the flanks of young trout and salmon, which usually fade in the second year of life. Some fish behaviourists believe they play a role in visual recognition and status signalling among juvenile salmonids.

Once the fish settle into their territories and become aware of each other's social status, the underlying level of aggression tends to decrease. Brown trout fry, in particular, show a reasonable degree of respect of the territorial boundaries of other fish at such times, mainly using visual display when they do have disagreements. However when mixed with rainbow trout, the brown trout's well-ordered rules of engagement seem to break down and much more serious fights ensue. Rainbow trout are more active than juvenile brown trout. They tend to be less fixed to focal points near the streambed and more willing to pursue a prey item into the territories of their neighbours. As a consequence, they continually break the rigid territorial rules to which brown trout adhere, often ignoring or overlooking the brown trout's visual displays that serve as a warning to interlopers. The result is an escalation in number and seriousness of territorial disputes, which often involve chasing and nipping.

I mentioned earlier that temperature can influence species dominance. The various species of salmonids have different thermal preferences. For example, brown trout grow best at 14°C, when feeding on invertebrates, and they stop feeding and growing at 19°C, whereas the rainbow's temperature growth optima and maxima are about 2°C higher. These growth differences between the species result from differences in metabolic performance and activity at different temperatures. A further consequence is that rainbow trout are more aggressive and can out-compete brown trout at higher temperatures (15–20°C) and the reverse occurs at lower temperatures (<15°C). These thermal effects on species dominance can drive patterns in the spatial distribution of salmonids down rivers (most rivers get warmer as they flow downstream). For instance, brook trout are usually restricted to the small, cold headwaters of some South Island river catchments where they may be confined by competition with brown trout. They have lower temperature preferences than either brown or rainbow trout.

There are situations, and times in their life history, when trout lay aside their aggressive territorial instincts and seek the apparent camaraderie of schools. Schooling is particularly common by yearling trout in the big pools of large rivers late in summer. Possibly schooling offers these fish better chances of avoiding predators at a time in their life when they are seeking bigger water and are becoming too big to hide in the spaces under rocks.

So far I have confined my discussion to trout defending their feeding space. There is another situation in which aggressive interaction is a significant feature in the lives of trout and salmon: spawning. On the spawning grounds, male salmonids, in particular, become very aggressive, regularly fighting other males. Females also show some aggression on the spawning grounds, but only to other females and only after they have finished spawning. Their interest is in defending their redds from being dug up by later spawning females. After about a week of this vigil, female trout lose interest and move back downstream to feed and recover from spawning.

Males confine their aggression to other males, competing for the favours of females. The stakes are so high at this time that most aggressive interactions involve chasing and biting. Morphological changes accompanying spawning transform the heads of male salmonids to enhance their fighting prowess. These changes are most extreme in the Pacific salmons. Their heads become hideously shaped, with wicked curved jaws and big teeth, specifically designed to intimidate and injure their rivals. Some fights can be very serious and prolonged. I once saw two male rainbows in a small stream about one metre wide take turns at charging each other's flanks with such force that each propelled the other fish onto the bank. The force of such charges can be heard through the water to an observer on the bank. Male trout frequently charge each other head on and lock jaws, twisting and turning before breaking free. This may be one cause of jaw damage, in addition to hooking injury, often seen in old rainbow trout.

As we have seen, the social life of trout is not harmonious, but rather selfish and bitchy. It is the outcome of raw competition for life's essentials — food and sex. There is a saying that nature is red in tooth and claw. Perhaps "and in fin" should be added to that phrase.

Up and active – ripe for the picking [PHOTO: DAVID HALLETT]

Targeting mending kelts on the upper Tongariro [PHOTO: DAVID HALLETT]

In search of perfect water may mean gaining permission for access
[PHOTO: DAVID HALLETT]

Waiting for the hatch [PHOTO: DAVID HALLETT]

Minimal handling out of water is the secret to proper catch and release [PHOTO: DAVID HALLETT]

Some anglers will do anything to get to the best lie [PHOTO: ZANE MIRFIN]

Serenity in sight of the hut [PHOTO: ZANE MIRFIN]

Converging braids make wonderful trout lies [PHOTO: ZANE MIRFIN]

A Contest Of Minds

BY TONY ENTWISTLE

"The body and spirit suffer no more sudden visitation than that of losing a big fish, since, after all, there must be some slight transition between life and death. But with a big fish, one moment the world is nuclear and the next it has disappeared. That's all. It has gone. Poets talk about 'spots in time', but it is really fishermen who experience eternity compressed into a moment. No one can tell what a spot in time is until suddenly the whole world is a fish and the fish is gone." — Norman Maclean. *A River Runs Through It.*

Bob had gamely battled the slug for over an hour and his arms ached from the physical torture of maintaining continuous pressure on his uncompromising quarry. Physically and mentally exhausted, Bob and his #6 rod had been literally stretched to their limits. This trout had towed us a kilometre downstream from the point of hookup, but not before first surging untroubled, upstream for 200 more metres through the white water of a rapid. Now, as Bob sidestrained the huge beast through the shallow waters of the tail out towards my waiting net, we dared believe for the first time that we might finally land it. That was, so long as about 80cm and 7kg plus of trophy trout would fit into the net!

But it was not to be. Within less than 30 centimetres of the mouth the net the seemingly acquiescent giant suddenly erupted into life and with one explosive burst was gone. I hadn't even made a play for the trout and now with only a face full of water to show for Bob's effort, the fight was over and the great fish had disappeared. The fly still hung limply from the tippet and we were both devastated.

When you play a trout into the shallows for the first time, never presume that the fight is over. Big trout often save their best fight until the last and in what some anglers might fancifully consider the real "contest of the minds", (except trout have brains smaller than a pea), it is the combination of luck and management in the final landing phase that ultimately determines your success or failure.

But there's no need to feel sorry for Bob and me. Truth is, we have had our successes on other big fish, where luck was on our side or maybe we managed the "final phase" a little better, but after 40 years of trout fishing I am still learning.

For some anglers I know, actually landing the trout is not always important. Some, when anticipating returning a fish live to the water, would even prefer to lose it while it was fresh, rather than playing it to a standstill and risk releasing it to die later. However having said that, I have not met any anglers who feel satisfied after losing a truly big fish and so I suggest all developing anglers should treat the landing of "lesser" fish as a dress rehearsal for the "big one".

My guiding records show that the ratio of "trout landed" (netted, weighed and released) to "trout hooked" averages only 55%. To some anglers this might initially seem a little low, but with me a clear "take" is recorded as a hookup, and so this figure also includes all missed takes. Clearly however, losing trout is part of the sport and something we have to get used to. But what are some of the keys to better management in the landing of a trout that might help maximise the number we can truly lay claim to finally capturing?

Apart from the first few seconds in the initial panic phase of the fight, the landing phase is the time when most fish are lost. Frequently, inexperienced or impatient anglers lock up on the reel and try to rush the landing, but this latter phase may take the greatest patience to complete. It can be a cat and mouse phase of give and take, with the trout making repeated but decreasingly powerful runs, as the angler gives line before regaining control of the fish again. At this stage, some anglers have real difficulty in finishing the fight and resort to playing the fish to a standstill, often relying simply on walking the fish downstream until it is exhausted.

From the angler's perspective, the greatest danger of any extended fight is the prospect of the hook pulling out, or abrasion causing the tippet to break. But every angler should make a conscious effort to refine their landing technique with the aim of ending the fight as expeditiously as possible, so that the fish can be released in a fit state or despatched humanely.

A large part of successfully landing a trout is in the planning. Even before casting to a trout or fishing a piece of water, an experienced angler will have looked at the water and considered where the best potential landing situations will be. Quite often on rivers this will not be in the immediate vicinity of the anticipated hookup and might well require the angler to play their fish some distance downstream. Sometimes the best area is nothing more than a shallow eddy in the edge water behind a rock or some other obstruction. When trying to land really big fish, look for areas of shallows where the river flattens out or even splits into a shallow braid. Sometimes it is possible to utilise the bulk of the fish to try and strand it in these places. However, big fish generally don't like to get out of their depth and it may take patience and "encouragement" to move them into the shallows.

The landing phase is the time of capture and there are a number of options available to the angler to achieve this, including netting, beaching, tailing, or gilling.

Personally I always like to use a net because it facilitates faster landing, ensures less likelihood of physical damage to the fish from thrashing against rocks, and also makes for easier handling for release. What type of net is mostly a matter of personal preference, however all nets should have an ample net bag that should be made out of soft, knotless netting to protect against scale removal and damage to the fish's skin.

Timing is always a critical element when netting any fish and this is much harder to judge between an angler and an associate netter, than when netting a fish for oneself. In the guiding situation, I like to use a wide-mouthed fixed frame net. They are more rigid than folding nets and in among the rocks and boulders that characterise the rivers I guide on, the rigid frame is a plus when I have to make a stab to get under someone else's fish. Fixed frame nets do, however, have a tendency to get in the way and catch on just about everything, especially when you are pushing through the "shrubbery" that flanks a lot of our New Zealand rivers.

For my own fishing these days, I have gone back to using a folding frame net that, when sheathed in its scabbard, is much less likely to get tangled in things. The key to a useful folding net is its ease of use especially upon opening, when you also have your hands full trying to subdue a kilo or more of pissed off trout. It should lock quickly into the open position and have strong enough wings not to collapse upon netting the fish. The easiest and most efficient folding net I have used is an innovative New Zealand-made net called The Rusler. It is well designed and constructed and the best folding net I have found to date.

When netting a trout by yourself, it is necessary to get the fish close, unless you use an absurdly long-handled net. Some nets have extension handles that help, but even then if the leader is longer than three metres it will probably require the junction of the line and leader to be drawn in through the top rod guides. This means that care needs to be taken to make sure this join is relatively small and neat. Generally, I find a needle or nail knot most suitable when joining the leader directly to the line. There are also many leader loop systems available to facilitate loop-to-loop connections, of which the finest and supplest I have found are the Roman Moser Minicon leader connectors.

The relatively small indicators we use when nymphing our southern waters are not a problem and move easily through the guides.

With any landing technique, gaining control of the fish's head is the key to achieving the final capture. In the latter stages of playing a fish, use of a low side-angled rod to apply maximum sidestrain will help achieve this. At the point of netting, it is important to raise the rod high again and use increased upward pressure, enough so that the net can be slipped in under the belly of the trout. For bigger fish, it is best to try and slide them into the net headfirst. Always avoid trying to net a fish from behind, as this is commonly a recipe for disaster.

Landing fish when the angler cannot (or chooses not to) make the security of the bank requires some additional special skills and the use of a good net is essential. Trout will most often end up below the angler's position and so will be landed against the flow of the river. While this may at first appear impossible in fast water, the secret is to use the river flow to help. Swing the fish directly downstream, where the eddy is set up from the body breaking the current and play the trout up into this eddy by keeping the rod hand as low as possible, but with the rod tip straight up above.

The next step requires judgement and timing, but practice makes perfect. Play the fish close to within three to four metres and when it is directly downstream, drive the rod arm straight up. This will have the effect of popping the trout to the surface, at which point immediately draw the rod tip straight back upstream. Apply this upstream pressure too soon, before the trout has popped to the surface, and it will simply bolt. If the fish isn't lost, it will have to be played back into position all over again.

When the trout has popped to the surface, the hydraulics of the upstream pressure applied against the flow of the current will cause the fish to slide across the top of the water, creating a short moment to slip the net under it before the fish is able to dive again. Miss this moment and it's usually back to the drawing board! The manoeuvre takes some good technique, a strong wrist in the rod hand, and is by no means infallible, but it will work in the majority of cases.

Obviously large trout (2.5kg or better) are much harder to handle this way than smaller fish, but it's your call whether you want to stay and battle the fish out in the ripple, or make the wade back to the bank to find a more secure landing option. We are lucky in New Zealand to have such weighty issues to consider. In most other parts of the world, it is a simple matter of holding the weight of the trout under the forefinger of the rod hand and stripping them across the surface. What a nice problem to have!

The sight of an angler sticking his toe under a fish and booting it up the bank is regrettably still witnessed, but is thankfully increasingly rare these days, as anglers have grown to appreciate a lot more the value of their quarry (both large and small). However, the most common method used by New Zealand anglers to land their trout would, in all likelihood, still be "beaching".

For anglers using the long leaders and large indicators typical on the Tongariro (and many other North Island waters), beaching is practically a necessity, unless the angler has someone else available to help net the fish. Because the large indicators can't be drawn through the guides, anglers simply can't get their fish close enough to net them themselves.

While beaching is a perfectly good method to use when anticipating killing your catch, it poses a number of threats for trout that are intended for release, particularly on rocky riverbeds where damage can easily occur to gills or internal organs. Exposure to dry rocks, gravel, or even sand can also cause damage to the trout's covering of mucus (slime), which can then lead to the later development of fungal or other infections that will ultimately result in distress or worse for the fish.

Anglers considering releasing beached trout have an added responsibility to try and make sure everything goes perfectly and that there is minimal danger to the fish. Any damaged trout should be killed and kept for the table. If you have to beach a trout, there are some simple steps to try and minimise any distress and physical damage.

To safely beach a fish, try and find an area of very fine wet gravel or preferably, wet sand. Slide the fish until its head is just exposed from the water and hold the fish briefly at this point, which will usually have the effect of stunning the fish. Generally, the fish will roll onto its side and can then be slid right out of the water with continuous pressure. Any trout that is going to be released, however, should not be removed completely from the water.

If you cannot completely beach the fish, or you have to land it in among larger rocks or boulders, try drawing the trout's head just out of the water and holding it up against a rock or some other obstruction, which in essence "fixes" it there. Keep firm pressure on the fish's head and this will then give you a better chance of being able to move in and either tail or gill it.

To efficiently "tail" or "gill" a trout relies on the fish first being immobilised in the water, which will normally mean it is at least partially beached as just described.

Tailing usually applies to bigger trout and on many occasions may well be the most practical way to capture those really big fish. A common trick to help grip the trout when tailing, involves using a bit of stocking material, or the simple handkerchief wrapped around the hand. I often wear protective Lycra sun-gloves these days, which are also a great help for tailing. Because I always have a net with me, many fish are assisted into the net by a combination of tailing and netting.

Gilling is simply a matter of spreading the hand over the back of the trout directly behind the gill plates and then forcing the fingers into the gills. It is an efficient way of subduing smaller fish, but should be restricted to trout that are going to be killed, as it is very difficult to avoid some damage to the gas-exchange surfaces of the gills and quite often results in bleeding. If you gill them, keep them.

Having finally achieved the capture of the trout, there are a number of handling techniques that will further help minimise problems, while hooks are removed and preparations are made for photographs or release.

The greatest way to calm trout I have discovered is to place a hand directly in front of the fish's nose, covering both its eyes. There is seldom even any need to grip the trout at all at this point. The next step is to get control of the trout's tail and remove the hook. Gripping a trout's tail is a matter of applying pressure to the upper and lower surfaces of the tail, in the knuckle area formed just at the junction of the caudal fin and body. This is best achieved using the joint of the thumb and the first joint of the forefinger. Avoid trying to grip the sides of the tail, as the trout will slip out of your fingers every time. Before attempting anything else with the fish, I then try lifting it slightly to make sure I have a good grip. Remember to wet your hands before touching a trout, again as a precaution against damaging the mucus coating on the skin.

If I am satisfied with the grip, I will then draw the fish out of the net and roll it upside-down, which also has the effect of pacifying the fish. This then makes it very easy to slip the forceps into the trout's mouth to remove the hook, exercising care, of course, to avoid damage to the fish's gills and gillrakers. This should all be done without removing the trout's head from the water.

If you have to lift the fish completely out of the water, maybe for a photograph or to carry it a short distance into deeper water to release it, take care not to squeeze the internal organs in the belly region back from the head. These can be easily damaged. If you have the correct grip on the tail it will simply be enough to slide the free hand with the fingers facing forward, under the belly and between the pectoral fins. This will effectively balance the fish at this point making it possible to lift it safely for a short time from the water. When taking a photograph, do all the preparation of positioning, framing, and focussing before lifting the trout from the water, and put the fish back in the water between photographs. Placing your hands over the eyes of the fish will continue to keep it calm during this time.

Landing a trout, especially a big one, is that nervous hell between the hard physical effort of playing the fish and the final ecstasy of consummation in the ultimate capture. It is the moment when angling dreams are so often fulfilled or shattered and is not an exact science, but rather an accumulation of experience grown out of knowledge earned from prior successes and failures — that good old "school of hard knocks".

It would have been Susan's first really big trout and, as with most other big trout, it had given her a punishing struggle. We had hooked the trout on a nymph, using a large dry fly as an indicator and looked all set to net it safely. But just as Susan drew the trout to the surface and I started sliding the net under it, I felt the dry fly bite into my shoulder.

There I was, locked firmly between my client concentrating for all she was worth on maintaining pressure, and four kilos of slippery muscle trying hard to go the other way. As I tried to lift the fish, "separation distance" proved to be exactly equal to the distance between the dry fly firmly embedded in my shoulder and the nymph in the trout's mouth. The fish balanced precariously briefly on the lip of my net before snapping the tippet with a final flick and disappeared, leaving poor Susan battling with a visibly distressed guide instead.

American writer, Verlyn Klinkenborg, describes the emotion of finally capturing a New Zealand trout: "Sooner or later you land one and everybody convenes on the river's edge, you, the guide, the trout coming head up to the net in a final shower of spray. You free the teeth from the bag, the hook from the jaw. With wet hands holding the fish against the current, you look at what you've caught... These fish are not just big; they are the healthiest, most beautiful trout you have ever touched. You release them, they flood their dive tanks, wriggle once, and are gone... you glimpse the final appeal of New Zealand angling.

"Wildness is not a state of being, but a principle of action. Clear water favours neither the angler nor the fish, though the angler thinks otherwise. A big trout is wilder than a small trout, and more demoralizing when spooked. The angler was never a fish, though the trout is always a hunter. A trout expects trouble, though the angler wants sport. A trout in hand is the muscular instant that is always vanishing, taking your life away with it..."

In The Guts

BY ROSS MILLICHAMP

Love it or hate it, the rivermouth is the scene that comes to people's minds when salmon fishing is mentioned. Lines of tightly packed anglers all queuing up for their turn at salmon that are due to run the gut that day. To most freshwater anglers, this scene is a long way from their idea of a relaxing day in the outdoors. However, the crowds suggest that there must be more to this form of salmon fishing than meets the eye.

Salmon spend most of their adult lives at sea, out of reach of recreational anglers. They hatch in freshwater, but enter the ocean before they are big enough to interest even the most ardent salmon anglers. Where they go during their two to three years at sea is a mystery. Even commercial fishermen can do little to solve the puzzle. All they can tell us is that salmon turn up in what appear to be "staging areas" a month or two prior to running the rivers. The rivermouth represents the place where the recreational salmon fishery begins. A stock of fish, which is insignificant when spread around the waters off the east coast of the South Island, merges into something meaningful at the rivermouths.

The principle reason why rivermouth salmon fishing is so popular is because it is a very productive place to fish. Surveys suggest that up to 75% of salmon caught in the Rangitata River are caught at the rivermouth. In seasons when river flows and the mouth shape are less suitable for rivermouth fishing, the catch may be lower, but it is never a location to be treated lightly.

The presence of hut settlements and camping grounds adjacent to almost every significant salmon fishing rivermouth is further evidence of their popularity and importance.

Rivermouth salmon angling can be split into two distinct disciplines — surf fishing and gut fishing. Surf fishing involves casting into the surf adjacent to the place where the river flows into the sea. Although surf fishing is a highly productive technique, it relies on rare weather conditions to come to fruition. Gut fishing takes place at the point where the river narrows just prior to entering the sea and is available just about every day the river is fishable. If surf fishing is the banquet, gut fishing is the bread and butter.

The guts of the various salmon riversmouths vary widely. The mouth of the Waimakariri River is more than 200 metres wide and not a "gut" in the true sense. At the other end of the scale are rivers like the Waiau, Hurunui, Opihi, and Orari, which have rivermouths as narrow as 30m, where all of the water can be easily covered with a short cast.

Whatever the geography, the principle attraction of all gut fishing is that the entire run of salmon must go past at some point during the season.

The typical salmon river empties into a lagoon before entering the sea. The lagoon is formed by a narrow shingle spit thrown up by the waves, which causes the river water to slow down and bank up. The place at which the spit is breached is constantly changing as the river and surf battle each other for dominance. The factors that affect the route salmon take while travelling through the gut change dramatically on every tide. Salmon seem to move quickly through the rough, disturbed waters where the river and sea meet, but reduce speed as soon as they reach the first taste of slower water. At times, they will pause here before moving out of the gut and into the lagoon proper. These are the prime places to catch salmon in the gut. The easiest way to identify these resting areas is to look for the place where the water profile changes from being angled to being flat. If you look at the gut in the last few metres before it enters the ocean, you will notice that the water surface is angling downhill. Turn and follow the river upstream until you can see the place where the surface flattens out. This is the place where salmon will most likely be caught. Going through this exercise, rather than heading straight for the place where they were caught the previous day, is well worthwhile.

Movement of salmon through the gut is affected by the tide. At low tide, the gut will be narrow, fast flowing and not attractive for salmon migration, particularly in the smaller rivers. But as the tide rises, the gut will widen, slow down and the salmon will move. The best fishing is when the tide has reduced the current speed, but not overcome it altogether. The fish will be forced to swim at the bottom of the deepest channel, where the current speed is slowest. At high tide, the gut may become so wide and so slack that the current will no longer keep the salmon together and the chances of putting a lure in front of one are not great. Not all rivers fish best on the incoming tide. The most notable exception is the Waimakariri, which as I have already mentioned, has a very different geography to other rivermouths. The Waimakariri fishes best on the top half of the outgoing tide, as it is the only time when there is enough current to group the salmon together.

The dramatic change in water depth and speed over a tidal cycle means that gut anglers have to put up with constantly changing fishing conditions. As the tide is starting to make, they will have to fish right on the bottom of a fast flowing channel. A lead weight up to 55 grams may be needed, in addition to a zed spinner or Colorado spoon, in these conditions. As the tide rises, the angler will have to reduce the amount of added weight, so they can fish the bottom without becoming constantly snagged. As the tide approaches high and the current dissipates, the salmon will no longer be forced to swim on the bottom. In these conditions, a light zed spinner, which has plenty of action, will do better than a heavy lure dragging the bottom.

Dealing with the vagaries of a constantly changing fishing environment is one obstacle for the gut angler; dealing with the number of other anglers is another. In my experience, the gut features higher angler densities than any other fishing location.

There is little point in fishing here if you don't enjoy the presence of your fellow anglers. Many anglers cannot understand the attraction of rivermouth fishing. They fish for relaxation and the idea of sharing the fishing spot with hoards of other anglers is abhorrent. Others see the crowds as the main attraction and seem to revel in it. Salmon fishing often involves long hours of toil without reward. Spending that time in the presence of your mates cannot be a bad thing. In my opinion, if you have not experienced the pandemonium of a busy day in the gut, you have not experienced all that salmon fishing has to offer.

The only reason that this many anglers can fish so close together without major confrontations is because there are a number of unwritten rules about how to behave. The best way to learn the rules is to spend time at a rivermouth and observe what goes on. The most difficult rule to come to terms with is how much space is required to enter the middle of a line of anglers. My opinion is that you can only enter the line if the anglers on either side do not have to move to accommodate you. Another rule relates to the tenure of your position in the line. It is generally accepted that you can return to your spot after landing a fish, changing a lure, or having a break. If a fish is hooked, any angler who has the potential to tangle with it, or get in the way of the angler, should retrieve their line and get out of the way. Most important is to fish in a similar fashion to other anglers. If you cast a similar distance with a similar type of lure and retrieve at the same rate as other anglers, you have less chance of getting tangled. As soon as you try to do anything different, the trouble will start. For example, if someone starts to fish with a feathered lure among anglers using spinning tackle, there will be problems due to the different way the lures behave in the current.

Landing fish is one of the real challenges of rivermouth angling. The crowded conditions mean that you do not have the same freedom to strike and set the hook into the fish that you have upriver. Sharp hooks and a short sideways strike are all that you can do to ensure the hook is well set. Once a fish is hooked, it is important to let your fellow anglers know, including those on the other side of a narrow gut. Experienced rivermouth anglers are not shy in telling others that they have a fish on! It is important to keep as close to the fish as possible throughout the fight. This way other anglers will have a clear idea of where the fish is and should get out of your way. Despite your best efforts, it is almost inevitable that someone will tangle with you during the fight, although most times this will not result in the fish being lost. Have another angler untangle the offending lure before it gets to your rod tip and there should be no problems. The best way of doing this is to have your helper take the other angler's lure in his hand, cut the line, and allow the tangle to undo.

Most novice salmon anglers are drawn to the rivermouth. This is in part due to the difficulty of locating water upriver and in part due to the opportunity the rivermouth offers to observe and learn from other anglers. Whether or not they catch a fish, fishing among other anglers gives novices a grounding in the basics of salmon angling. Perhaps because of the presence of learner anglers, the rivermouth is often not considered a serious fishing location. However, successful rivermouth anglers are among the most skilled salmon anglers there are. They not only have to contend with the vagaries of salmon runs, but with the presence of a heap of other anglers as well. They do not have the opportunity to move through a piece of water, or to rest it like an upriver angler. At times, they are forced to fish from less desirable positions in the line because the best ones are taken. Despite these difficulties, a solid percentage of the salmon taken at each rivermouth is taken by a handful of local experts. They understand the effect of wind, tide, river flow, and surf on their beloved pile of stones and are able to spot any new water as it develops.

The rivermouth is the Wild West of the salmon fishery, because anything that is going to happen will happen there first. The salmon arrive in top condition and at their most vulnerable to angling. The only problem is that rivermouth anglers have no idea of when runs are going to turn up. Some factors suggest a run is more likely, but the only way to be there on the same day as the salmon is to put in consistent effort. Salmon seldom run for more than a day or two on end, so if you wait to hear of a run there is every chance that it will be over by the time you get there.

Catch And Release – Facts, Fiction, And The Future

BY ROGER YOUNG, CARL WALROND, AND
JOHN HAYES OF THE CAWTHRON INSTITUTE

To some anglers there is nothing more satisfying than landing a large trout, unhooking it, and then watching it cruise off to the nearest available cover. It feels great knowing that the fish may be there next time, or for the next angler. There is also something thrilling about holding a live, glistening, and vibrantly coloured fish in your hands. To some, this euphoric moment quickly fades with the colours of the trout if it dies. Feelings such as these have resulted in catch and release (C & R) becoming very popular in New Zealand over the last 10 years. The Cawthron Institute's research confirms that C & R has become commonplace. It has also shown support among anglers for mandatory C & R regulations for some backcountry rivers. Already there are C & R regulations on several rivers and lakes in Southland, Otago, North Canterbury, and Taranaki, and maximum size limits for trout on some parts of the Eastern, Hawke's Bay, and Wellington Fish & Game regions. Despite support for C & R, there is relatively little known about its success and the benefits and costs associated with it for our fisheries. There are many questions that can be asked. Will C & R work in all rivers? What are the chances that trout will survive after being released? Will released fish be affected in any other way? Will trout learn from being caught and become harder

"Walking the dog" [PHOTO: ZANE MIRFIN]

A very casual cast was this [PHOTO: ZANE MIRFIN]

Acrobatics from a wild brown [PHOTO: ZANE MIRFIN]

Two NZ favourites – a Hare & Copper and a white caddis
[PHOTO: LES HILL]

Wild flowers and fishing – is there a better combination?
[PHOTO: LES HILL]

Mayflies anyone? [PHOTO: LES HILL]

Man's best friend finds it all a bit tiring [PHOTO: LES HILL]

Hanging on in fast water [PHOTO: LES HILL]

to catch next time?

During the late 1990s, Carl Walrond surveyed anglers from Otago and Nelson/Marlborough to measure the levels of crowding on our backcountry rivers. He also looked at angling success and anglers' attitudes to various issues. This work forms part of Cawthron's backcountry river trout fisheries research programme jointly funded by the Foundation for Research, Science & Technology and Fish & Game New Zealand. One of the issues examined was C & R. Based upon returns from all angler diaries, 6830 out of 7408 trout (92%) were released after capture. Non-residents had higher release rates (98.8%) than resident New Zealand anglers (80%). Guided anglers, who were primarily non-residents, released a higher proportion of trout (99.6%) than unguided anglers (81%). Fish & Game New Zealand Otago Region found similar patterns on the Greenstone and Caples rivers where the proportion of trout released had increased from about 80% to 96% over the last decade.

The plea for voluntary C & R in fragile backcountry rivers is obviously being heard!

Before the study, we expected that very large trophy trout might be targeted by anglers and removed for subsequent taxidermy and mounting. However, there was no evidence for this in Walrond's results. Among all the angler diaries, the average weight of trout released was actually higher than those killed. Even among the heaviest 10% of fish (trophy size), there was no difference in average weight between trophy fish that were killed and released. Only 1% of trophy trout were killed, compared to 7.8% for the whole sample.

Another point raised in Walrond's questionnaire was whether anglers would support mandatory C & R regulation in some backcountry rivers.

The majority of anglers were in favour, with non-resident anglers more strongly in favour than resident anglers. A typical comment from American anglers was: "I can't believe that there aren't more C & R waters." This strong support for C & R regulations is interesting. Given that most trout are voluntarily released anyway, maybe anglers support regulation changes because they know it won't change their behaviour, and it ensures that others follow the lead they are already taking.

Despite the adherence to C & R in our backcountry rivers, and the support for mandatory regulations on some rivers, there isn't much information on the costs and benefits of it in New Zealand. Behavioural and habitat changes among fish that have been released may decrease their availability to anglers. Shifts in habitat occupied by trout to avoid disturbance may result in them taking up less profitable feeding locations and thus result in decreased growth rates and population carrying capacity. Fish & Game New Zealand Southland Region set up three experimental C & R zones on the Mataura, Oreti and Eglinton rivers. Results suggest an increase in trout abundance in the Mataura and Oreti C & R zones compared to neighbouring reaches with standard regulations. However, there has been no obvious effect of C & R in the Eglinton River. The reasons why C & R is successful in some rivers and not others are unclear, but may be related to the comparatively short length of the experimental C & R zones. Perhaps fish in the Eglinton are highly migratory and fish from elsewhere in the river quickly replace trout taken by anglers. Also, unlike the Mataura and Oreti, the Eglinton discharges into a lake from which additional recruitment is available. Another possibility could be that anglers are voluntarily returning most of their catch throughout the river and are thus diluting the contrast with the C & R zones.

Some clues relating to the success or failure of C & R regulations can be picked up from the results of research conducted overseas. C & R regulations are widely implemented in North America and as a result much of the information comes from there. Obviously, conditions in New Zealand are different from North America, but there are plenty of lessons that we can learn. The best examples of success with C & R regulations are with cutthroat trout, which are highly susceptible to angling. Rainbow trout are a little harder to catch, while most anglers find that brown trout are the most difficult to catch. For this reason, the response of brown trout to C & R is generally the least pronounced. Nevertheless, C & R has resulted in significant improvements to some brown trout fisheries.

Increases in catch rates from rivers with C & R regulations have been spectacular in many parts of North America. Larger average size fish have also been reported. Many of these fisheries were traditionally maintained by yearly releases of takeable-sized fish, but with the advent of C & R put-and-take tactics are no longer required. C & R regulations have not always been successful. In coldwater streams where low temperatures control fish growth and harsh winter conditions cause high natural mortality, the number of fish taken by anglers can be insignificant compared to natural death rates. Changes in fisheries regulations in these waters are unlikely to have much effect. C & R regulations in rivers with good juvenile recruitment have increased competition between individual trout and returned high catch rates of stunted fish — a situation we would want to avoid in New Zealand. The lesson here is that C & R should only be considered where angling pressure is likely to influence the trout population, and where trout density is naturally low. To some extent, the success of C & R depends on the effects anglers have on fish they release. Many anglers must wonder: "Will the fish that I've just released survive?" The general consensus from several studies is that more than 90% of fish will survive. Reports have been made of individual trout being caught and released up to 13 times in one season. In one section of the Yellowstone River, cutthroat trout are caught an average of 9.7 times during a season. No New Zealand river is fished this heavily yet, but these results show how durable trout can be. A further example of trout resilience is the survival rate of brown trout in radio-tracking studies. A recent study of the Wairau River showed that 95% of trout survived the trauma of being caught by anglers and the subsequent anaesthesia and surgical implantation of radio transmitters. The stress associated with this procedure would no doubt exceed that experienced by trout that are simply caught and released.

Not all fish that are released will survive. Fish that are hooked in the gills or stomach, as is often the case when using bait, bleed heavily and have lower survival rates than fish hooked in the mouth or corner of the jaw. Prolonged handling also decreases their chances of survival. After an exhausting period of "exercise", the last thing a trout needs is to be lifted out of their watery surroundings to an environment where they can't breathe. So those nice photos of a trout before release add to the stress experienced by the fish. Warm summer temperatures decrease survival among fish that are released, so particular care should be taken to quickly return trout to the water under these conditions.

Another interesting factor that affects survival upon release is the depth from which trout are caught. Clearly, this is not a problem in river fisheries, but in lakes the swim bladders of fish that are hauled to the surface may expand rapidly, resulting in internal injuries and buoyancy problems. Research by DoC at Turangi has shown that survival of rainbow trout in Lake Taupo decreases with increasing depth of capture. A North American study showed that survival of largemouth bass caught at depth could be improved by puncturing their swim bladder before release. The same procedure is now advocated for hapuka in New Zealand.

There have been many debates in North America about the use of barbed versus barbless hooks. Many believe that barbless hooks allow fish to be easily and quickly unhooked and returned to the water. However, early reviews of the barbed versus barbless hook issue showed no differences in mortality between hook types. More recent work has suggested that mortality rates were higher where barbed hooks were used, but others have questioned the strength of these claims. In fact, it is possible that barbless hooks are more harmful because they penetrate further into a fish's flesh. Overall, it seems likely that any differences in mortality between hook types are small and unlikely to affect survival rates in natural streams.

Even if a trout survives after being released, it may still be harmed by the experience. Physiological studies have shown an increase in the concentration of lactic acid and a decrease in energy reserves and oxygen in the blood of trout after exhaustive "exercise". Recovery from being caught may take a considerable amount of time — two to eight hours to reduce lactic acid to normal levels and up to 12 hours to restore energy reserves. Such physiological changes have the potential to limit the reproductive success of fish that have been caught and released many times. However, studies on Atlantic salmon have shown no difference in egg or sperm viability between fish that have been caught and released and those that were undisturbed.

Changes in trout behaviour after being caught and released are also likely. A laboratory-based study in North America found that brown trout stopped feeding for up to three days after being handled. Another study showed that C & R disrupted the dominance hierarchies of wild cutthroat trout in an Idaho river. The largest and dominant fish were the most vulnerable to capture and in three out of four cases the released fish lost its preferred feeding position to another trout that had not been caught. The authors also found that catchability decreased over time for hatchery rainbow trout, suggesting that the fish were learning to avoid being caught. They also observed a small increase in the proportion of fish caught every three to four weeks, perhaps indicating that such learning and memory only lasts for approximately a month. The same study also showed that wild cutthroat and rainbow trout were more susceptible to angling in a river that was closed to fishing than in other rivers where constant angling pressure was applied. This may again indicate that trout are able to learn to avoid being hooked, but may also be the result of the "easy" fish being caught and removed from the stream where angling was allowed. From 1998 to 1999, we have also been addressing the question: "Do trout become more difficult to catch after being caught and released?"

Preliminary information from an experiment we conducted on a relatively unfished brown trout population in Kahurangi National Park showed that the trout responded to fishing pressure by hiding more and becoming more difficult to catch.

Fisheries aren't just about fish — the response of anglers to C & R is also important. In general, most studies from North America have shown an initial decrease in angling use after C & R has been imposed, followed by an increase several years later in response to increased catch rates and fish size. This increase in angling pressure has reached extremes in several cases and there are now major overcrowding problems, with limits set on the number of anglers allowed on certain stretches of water. Anglers in New Zealand may also be drawn to C & R zones expecting bigger fish, higher trout densities, and better catch rates. According to Maurice Rodway, manager of Fish & Game New Zealand Southland Region, anglers' response to the experimental C & R zones in this region has generally been positive. There is some evidence of an increase in angling pressure in the Oreti and Mataura C & R zones, but this is difficult to separate from the general trend of increasing use of New Zealand's backcountry river fisheries. A similar response was found on the Lochy (New Zealand's first C & R regulated river) and Routeburn rivers. Compliance with the regulations has been excellent and no overcrowding problems related to the C & R regulations have been identified. Angler encounter rates from Walrond's study show no differences between C & R rivers and rivers with standard regulations.

Although the North American C & R research is useful, we must remember that New Zealand fisheries are unique in many ways. Angling pressure on many rivers in North America is far higher than that currently experienced in New Zealand. So the impacts of anglers on fish populations are more pronounced. On the other hand, North American streams often have large numbers of small fish, whereas New Zealand's backcountry rivers have comparatively low densities of large fish. So, despite lower angling pressure in New Zealand, the impacts may still be significant. While voluntary changes in angling philosophy are likely to continue to be the major factor influencing future trends in angling, regulations relating to C & R, and also access restrictions, may have increasing importance in the future. Angling pressure in New Zealand's backcountry rivers appears to be increasing. In response to this pressure, C & R will undoubtedly remain popular among anglers in New Zealand and will be increasingly important in maintaining acceptable catch rates of large fish in the future.

C & R Dos and Don'ts

Top New Zealand trout fishing guide Tony Entwistle has long been a believer in catch and release, although he harbours some reservations about mandatory C & R. To his way of thinking, establishing regulated C & R sections on rivers is like "sending an invitation to flyfishers to hammer that water".

"Most anglers wrongly will consider any designated section of river set up as C & R water to be positively loaded with fish," he says. "So while fisheries managers may be trying to protect a particular fishery with mandatory C & R, it is possible they may instead be increasing angling pressure on already delicate waters.

"I see C & R not as a regulation, but as an ethic," says Entwistle, who probably concurs with what prolific American angling author Robert Traver once wrote: "One way to get the dope on a man is to watch him fish...his technique or lack of it... possibly more subtle clues to the inner man, such as how he handles a fish once caught, including how he removes, and returns it..."

Entwistle has compiled a list of guidelines to help ethical anglers properly "remove and return trout". He recommends:

- using the heaviest strength tippet possible to effectively catch and fight fish

- using barbless hooks, which can be optional, but which facilitate easier release

- learning to play fish quickly and efficiently with correct sidestrain

- using a strong landing net

o   exercising extreme care in handling, i.e. wetting your hands before touching fish, not removing the fish from water too long, avoiding squeezing the fish, and keeping fingers away from gills

o   always replacing trout in gently flowing current, allowing it to revive itself when releasing large fish, always providing support, but never moving a fish back and forth in the current

o   on release, giving the fish a firm forward push into the current

o   being willing to kill any fish that doesn't look likely to survive.

Trolling Made Easy

BY PETER CHURCH

The reel starts screaming, the fish jumps behind the boat, trying to throw the hook. Nervous hands wait for the first mad run to stop, then they coax the line gently back onto the reel, always ready to give line if the fish runs again. The landing net dips and a struggling trout is lifted on board. Congratulations are offered to the lucky angler and everybody on board settles down to reset the lines. This is a common scene throughout the country's lakes. New Zealand is blessed with an abundance of lakes that offer great opportunities to catch quality trout by trolling.

Trolling is a very popular way of trout fishing. It provides a good way to introduce people to the sport and also is a superb way for the whole family to enjoy trout fishing.

Trolling can be very productive at times, especially when water or weather conditions concentrate the trout. Typically as summer warms the water, trout will move deeper, seeking cooler water. Trolling is a way of getting a line down to these fish. The wind can also play a big part in where the fish feed, concentrating bait fish in areas where it is only possible to reach them by boat. Trolling allows the versatile angler to follow the seasonal movement of trout through the year.

The newcomer to trolling can be confused by some of the terms used. One of these is harling. Harling is a technique that is very popular on Taupo and Rotorua lakes. It is simply shallow trolling. Usually the lure or fly is fished within three metres of the surface.

Most people when talking about trolling are referring to fishing the line deeper by using wire, lead line, or LED lines depending on what the local regulations will allow.

One of the nice features of freshwater trolling is that any boat is suitable. Boat speed is critical for successful trolling. The boat must be able to go speeds of between 1mph and 2.5mph. Using the auxiliary motor is now common practice. This allows for very accurate speed control and is better for the main motor. Long periods of running at low revs can result in oiling up of the motor or burning out sparkplugs. If the boat is still going too fast, a sea anchor can be dragged on a short line to help slow it down.

A bucket can even be used. The disadvantage of this system is that the sea anchor must be pulled in quickly when a hookup happens to avoid tangles. A wide range of rods can be used for trolling. Usually a short rod, around two metres, is favoured. Shorter rods are easier to handle in a boating situation. The best type rod has a stiff butt section and a soft tip action. The soft tip action will help stop the hook being torn from the mouth of the trout during the strike and landing. There are some good, reasonably priced rods on the market specifically made for trout trolling.

The reel is the important part of the outfit. There are two requirements in a reel for trolling — a good drag system and large line capacity. The type of reel used is a matter of personal choice and budget. A large centre pin reel with a star drag system on the front is the simple option. The advantage of these reels is they are simple to use and with very few moving parts to go wrong, little trouble can arise. The disadvantages are the line must be spread by hand during the wind in and care must be taken playing the fish, allowing it to run when it wants by removing hands from the reel.

The other option is to use a conventional overhead reel with level wind, slipping clutch, and geared ratio for a faster wind in. These reels are becoming popular in freshwater trolling, particularly with women anglers, because of the fast retrieve of the line, which is a major advantage over a centre pin reel. The slipping clutch should also result in less break-offs during the landing of a fish. Of course, there is a catch to these extra features — they cost more.

Get the best reel the budget can stand and maintain it well.

The type of line used depends on two factors — how deep one wants to fish, and the local regulations. The three standard lines used are LED, lead line, and wire. LED lines, with the addition of a Deep Water Express line, will sink to the same depth as lead line. Wire line will sink deeper. All three lines can be purchased on standard 100 metre spools. On some lakes around the country, lead lines or wire may not be used. If possible, get the tackle shop to splice a loop at one end of the line to attach the leader to, and splice the backing on to the main line.

All reels should have at least 100 metres of backing. The backing acts as a reserve for when that big fish we all dream about hits.

It will also fill the reel spool so that the maximum amount of line is retrieved on every revolution of the spool. Use a braided backing of around 15kg breaking strain.

A piece of equipment that is often overlooked until the last minute is a landing net. A net with a long or extending handle is a real advantage and can save losing fish at the side of the boat. Use a soft cotton net bag if possible. The soft material will not damage the fish if it is to be returned.

The last accessory seen on most boats today is a depth sounder or fish finder. These instruments come in a wide range of sizes to suit most boats and can make trolling much easier, but they don't guarantee to make fish bite. Apart from the obvious fish finding function, the sounder helps to run the lines at a consistent depth just off the lake bottom where the lures are most effective. Most sounders also have a speed reading on the display, which helps the skipper keep the speed in the right range for line depth and lure movement.

Now that all the gear is packed on board, what to do? Before setting the lines for the first time, pull some line off and run the lures beside the boat. Watch the lure movement. This is what attracts the trout. Experiment with the boat speed until the lures move the most. This is the best speed at which to troll. Take a note of the speed. For most lures, the optimum speed is 1.5mph to 2mph.

Now set the lines. Starting in deep water, speed up the boat to around 4mph, then pull out some line behind the boat. Most reels have a free spool function on the drag system, so once a few metres of line is out the rest will free spool out. Watch out for a backlash.

For best results, the lures should be fished as close to the lake bottom as possible, so how much line is run out depends on the depth to be trolled. At 1.8mph, 100 metres of lead line or LED with Deep Water Express will sink between 40–45 feet. Wire line fished at the same speed will go down 60–65 feet.

Lead line comes with every 10 metres marked a different colour. So, based on 100m of lead line being trolled at 1.8mph, six colours will go down 24 feet. Of course, going faster will lift the lines higher in the water. Experienced trollers mark the LED and wire lines so that the amount of line out can be determined easily.

Now slow down the boat to trolling speed and set the strike drag. Finding the correct setting may take a little experience. The correct drag will have enough resistance to set the hook in the mouth while still allowing the fish to run on the strike. Check the drag by hand. There is no need to strike the fish hard on the take. If the drag is set well, the momentum of the boat and the weight of the line will secure a good hookup.

The number of lines fished at once depends on the size of the boat. For example, boats up to 18ft will run two lead lines if rod tips are kept well apart. If a third line is used, a shallow or shorter line in the middle of the boat will avoid tangles. The idea is to run the lines at different depths if multiple lines are used. Most bad tangles occur when the boat is turning. The line running on the inside of the curve will slow down and drop deeper in the water. The outside line will speed up and cut across the curve, catching the inside line. To avoid this, speed up the boat a little and make a wide gentle turn.

Speeding up the boat, or putting a little curve in the line can result in a hookup. Any change in lure movement may attract the fish. Many trollers will deliberately make small alterations in the boat speed. For example, the boat can be slowed right down, sinking lines into a hole, then sped up, pulling lures away from the bottom. This type movement can be hard for a trout to resist.

At some stage, it is likely a lure will get caught on the lake bottom. Logs or rocks are the usual culprits. The best way to retrieve the gear is to back up the boat slowly, winding in the slack line until the boat is on the other side of the snag. Very often the lure will come free during this manoeuvre. If not, pull firmly on the line. Sometimes this will clear the snag. Always check the hook point after being snagged and sharpen the point if necessary.

When playing and landing the fish, the normal rules apply. Keep a tight line on the fish at all times, being prepared to let it have its head at any time. There are a couple of tips that make landing the fish easier. Always wind in the other lines quickly to stop tangling, or snagging the bottom. On calm days, cut the motor quickly after the hookup to reduce the drag on the line. However, on windy days if trolling into the wind, keep the boat going forward very slowly to help keep the line tight on the fish. Many fish are lost right at the side of the boat, so be prepared to let the fish have line as it sees the boat for the first time and panics.

Arriving at the lake edge for the first time to go fishing can be a bit daunting. Where are the fish?

Trout like structure. It helps to imagine the lake without water. Look for any dropoffs, reefs, rocky points, and weed beds. These areas will concentrate the trout food and so become consistent feeding areas. A marine map, if available, is a great help and many of the more popular trolling lakes have good information booklets to help the beginner locate these areas.

Dropoffs are worked best by trolling along just on the deep water, then coming up on the drop off in a gentle curve, lining up along the edge at the right depth for the line being used. Then follow the contour of the dropoff as far as possible. This is where a sounder is a great asset, making it possible to follow the dropoff at a consistent depth, running the lures close to the bottom. If a sounder is not used, it is possible to do this by watching the water colour. On a sunny day, the water goes a lighter colour as it shallows. For example, 100 metres of lead line can be fished where the water changes colour from deep blue to green.

On a dull day, this will not work, so most trollers have a series of landmarks worked out to help. The use of landmarks also helps in identifying hot spots. If a fish is hooked, it is worth marking the spot with a feature on the shore. Very often fish will be hooked in the same spot in future.

Skippers who catch fish consistently usually have a system worked out, working a trolling run carefully, then checking the lines to make sure there is no weed or rubbish on the hook before running back through the run in the opposite direction. Working a hot spot will in the long run produce more fish than blindly setting sail across a lake.

Checking the lines at regular intervals can be quite important. There is nothing more unproductive than dragging a lump of weed around a lake for an hour.

The wind is the other factor influencing the fishing. Troll the sheltered shoreline. This not only makes boat handling easier and increases passenger comfort, it is where the fish will often feed. Long periods of wind from one direction will often concentrate bait fish seeking calm water.

Walking into a tackle shop to buy trolling lures can be confusing. Some ranges of lures have 50 to 60 different colours. Remember, the key to catching fish trolling is correct lure depth and speed, not the number of red spots on a lure. There are a few basic lure types available in New Zealand — Toby, Tasmanian Devil, Cobra, and Flatfish. A selection of these lures in black, green, white, and yellow is a good starting point. There are times when a lure, such as a Hot Pink Cobra, is the only colour the fish will look at, so it is worth having a few odd ball colours in the box.

How well the lure works in the water is dependent on the design and the way it is rigged on the leader. Most lures are designed with a curve in the body, which causes an erratic action as the water passes. A 10–15 metre leader is important for two reasons — keeping the lure well away from the heavy line, and the longer leader will allow the lure to move freely. Using 8lb or 10lb breaking strain leader will also help the lure action by reducing the water resistance.

Cobras and Tasmanian Devils can also be rigged to give the lure more movement. New lures have a wire running through the middle of the body. Remove the wire and run the leader through the middle. Tie a split ring with a hook on the end of the leader to secure the lure. A final touch can be added, using a teaser tied on the hook to give more colour and action. The split ring teasers are available from many tackle shops. When using this rig, tie a swivel in the leader two metres from the lure. This will help stop line twist in the leader.

In some areas, two lures or flies can be used. Using a combination of lure and fly is common. There are two ways of tying these rigs. The first is to tie a fly on a short piece of nylon from the back of the lure hook. The second is to run a fly on the leader above the swivel.

Always observe good boating safety. Let somebody know your plans, check the weather, and take and use lifesaving equipment. Use common sense. Trolling in the middle of some of the country's larger lakes in a 3m dinghy is not recommended. Many of these lakes are very changeable and turn from flat calm to rough in a matter of minutes. That long, cold swim can be fatal.

Trolling is a great excuse to enjoy some of the beautiful places in New Zealand. Get out and try it.

The Business End of Jigging

BY DAVID MOATE

One of the many great things about fishing is the variety of angling methods we can use to catch fish and enhance our sport. Advancements in one aspect of fishing are often picked up by adventurous anglers and used to improve, or even create other sports fishing opportunities. Non-stretch superbraid fishing lines, which have revolutionized deep water fishing in the ocean, have done the same for deep water freshwater fishing by significantly improving the effectiveness and sporting attributes of jigging.

Jigging for trout is certainly not a new method. It was originally called ledgering and involved anchoring in a suitable location and casting a spinner out, letting it flutter to the bottom, and then working it back to the boat. This method, as well as the first attempts at jigging with small metal lures, was successful but not popular. Nylon stretches and significantly reduces the ability to feel what is happening in the depths that greatly detracts from the sporting aspects of jigging. The non-stretch superbraid lines have now completely turned this around, enabling us to use lighter gear, feel even the most tentative of bites, accurately judge depths, and work jigs and flies effectively. Today, jigging for trout is very sporting with the tackle being much lighter and more sensitive than flyrods required to fish deep water. Its also very productive, taking its share of the catch and more than its share of the larger, well conditioned specimens. It also requires skill and

Shoreline cruisers are incredible fun [PHOTO: LES HILL]

Waiting for the take on a high country tarn [PHOTO: LES HILL]

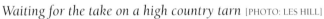

A prize is returned safely [PHOTO: LES HILL]

Always bring the fish to the net, not the net to the fish [PHOTO: LES HILL]

Mastering big water [PHOTO: ZANE MIRFIN]

A Harihari spring creek brown about to go back [PHOTO: BOB SOUTH]

Dry fly fishing the Tasman River with Mt Cook as the backdrop
[PHOTO: DAVID HALLETT]

Being cautious on the banks of one of the tiny lakes around Tekapo
[PHOTO: DAVID HALLETT]

experimentation and costs less than most other fishing tackle. Everyone in the family can quickly master the technique.

A variety of jigging rods and reels are available to match your budget and requirements. You can purchase outfits that will be suitable for both trout and light saltwater jigging, but outfits designed to do a specific job are the best as with all fishing tackle. Fortunately, trout jigging outfits are not expensive, with around $100 getting you good equipment. An overhead reel, which has a fast retrieve, level wind, smooth drag and a push lever to quickly place in and out of gear, is vital. Flip feature on the gear lever is handy after the initial drop, for quick re-adjustments and for preventing over-spooling. Make sure the reel also has a free spool drag setting so you can set it for the weight used, ensuring a smooth quick drop. Finally, make certain the reel fits your hand comfortably. It's a good idea to measure how much line each turn of the reel actually retrieves so you can very accurately judge how far off the lakebed you are fishing. The rod needs to be light, sensitive, and one that loads well under the weight of a fish, but with a tip that does not overload when lifting the jig or weight. You do not need a long rod for trout jigging, as you are not moving the lures much. A shorter rod is easier on the wrist — try 1.5m to 1.7m with casting weights from 25 to 60 grams. Select 100 metres of quality non-stretch superbraid line from 4–8kg. The fusion and fireline brands are recommended ahead of other superbraids. They are stiffer and do not tip-wrap or tangle as easy. Fill the first half of the reel drum with normal nylon, and then add the superbraid line. This will help retain rapid retrieve, help the level wind keep the superbraid line from slipping over or under itself, and will not overfill the reel, which also prevents over-runs and tangles. Non-stretch superbraid lines are essential for jigging. They transmit the slightest touch to you whether it be a fish or the jig hitting the bottom. You can even feel the jig fall over and touch the bottom and even hook small smelt and bullies that often nibble the lures. Because there is no stretch in the line, you will require a lighter drag setting on the reel than you would for nylon. Also try to keep the rod and line at right angles when playing a fish, or you will break the nylon leader, or most likely tear the hook out. When tying knots in superbraid or to nylon, you must double both sections and add several more turns in the knot. The best knot to use is the uni-knot to attach hooks or swivels and the double uni-knot to join superbraid to superbraid, or superbraid to nylon. To prevent over-runs, always rewind with tension and drop or cast with thumb tension and control. If you do get a tangle, do not pull any ends tight as you may not be able to get any knots undone. Keep everything loose and carefully unwind the tangle. Be aware, too, that superbraid lines can cut through your skin if you pull it quickly and firmly.

Once the gear is all set up, the business end of a trout jigging rig needs attention. Two variations of rigs are commonly used. First is the metal jig on the bottom with one or two flies above. Join to the end of the superbraid, using a uni-knot, two metres of nylon slightly lighter in breaking strain than the superbraid. Attach a size 14 swivel and another one metre of nylon. Further attach a size 14 snap swivel or a jig. Attach to the top eye of the top swivel a 30cm long dropper of nylon slightly lighter than the main trace and a size two fly. The second method is the lead weight on the bottom with two or three flies above. Join to the end of the superbraid, using a uni-knot, two metres of nylon slightly lighter in breaking strain than the superbraid. Attach a size 14 swivel and another metre of nylon. Attach another 40cm of nylon and a size 14 snap swivel. Clip on a suitable weight, or hookless jig to the snap swivel. Attach to the top eye of both swivels a 30cm dropper of nylon slightly lighter than the main trace and size two flies. A jig without a hook, instead of a lead weight, is another option for this rig.

Keeping the main trace nylon lighter than the super braid will ensure you do not lose everything on a deep snag. Swivels are better than dropper knots as they substantially reduce tangles and help stop the flies and jigs spinning. Jigs with a wire loop on the nose can be attached via the snap swivel, or hollow ones have the body sliding up the nylon. Placing a plastic bead between the jig body and hook will protect the nylon. Small three-way swivels are an improvement to a single swivel, further reducing spinning and keeping the flies away from the trace. On a single swivel, pull the dropper knot up to the trace knot to further help keep the dropper away from the main trace. If you have a missed strike, you can see which fly was hit because the knot will be pulled down. The best lead weights are teardrop-shaped with a swivel attached, as they drop very quickly without spinning and give a good solid thump when bottom is found. Another option is to use ball sinkers thread onto heavy copper wire with a loop formed on one end. Using a jig instead of a lead weight gives more action to the flies and the jig adds its share of flash and movement. But beware that it can tangle the rig on the drop and is slower to reach the bottom.

Jigs weighing from 15–45 grams are commonly used, depending on depth and drift speeds. The most productive colours of metal jigs are green and yellow, red and white, or silver. If you are using the lead jig heads with attached rubber bodies, then black, pearl, or the shade patterns are proven catchers. For jigging at night, try lumo beads on the trace above the jig, or lumo rubber squids slipped onto a hook.

Jig flies, used in water depths from seven to 20 metres can be standard sized patterns, but once you get deeper than 20 metres better results will be on size 2 patterns. All popular patterns will work, especially ones with lots of pulsating movement that do not spin. Patterns copying smelt, bullies, and koura are the most productive and can be mixed. Keep the bully or koura patterns on the bottom dropper and smelt on the top dropper. At night in deep water, or on dull days, use patterns with lumo paint or strips incorporated, or add lumo beads to the dropper. Pattern selection is as important in jig fishing as flyfishing, so if patterns are not working on the day experiment and note the results for future use.

You can successfully jig fish for trout in any type of boat — big or small. If the boat sits low in the water and drifts slowly, all the better. The boat needs two essential pieces of equipment to be able to jig effectively — a sounder (fish finder) and a sea anchor. A top quality colour sounder will undoubtedly be an advantage if you can interpret the information into finding trout. But any basic models will be fine, as it's mainly the bottom contours, depth, and water temperature information you need. Do not get hung up on hoping the sounder will show you schools of trout. Instead, note the depths at which the fish icons are and, if you do find large concentrations, it will usually be baitfish, although trout will not be far away. Large fish icons stacked up three or more deep indicate trout and all information about their depth and location is worth checking. A nylon parachute style sea anchor that is quick to deploy and retrieve is ideal to slow down boat drift and help manipulate the drift direction.

It's possible to simply start jig fishing anywhere in a lake, but like all fishing spending time locating fish pays dividends. Water temperature is one of the keys to locating trout in a lake. From late December to May water temperature increases and creates layers of water. Cold water is heavy, so it sinks to the bottom, while the warm lighter water stays on top. Separating these two layers is a narrow band of water called the thermocline, which stays the same temperature all the time. As the bottom water becomes oxygen-depleted and the top layer becomes too warm, trout are forced to spend most of the time in the thermocline. Good quality sounders show the thermocline and even how thick it is. Average sounders will not show this, but by increasing the machine's sensitivity setting and using the fish icons you will soon see where it is located, as the sounder picks up the concentrations of fish life in and around the thermocline. From June to early December, trout can be found throughout the lake depths because the water is the same temperature at all depths. Much of the trout's food is found on the lakebed living in the weed and structure. Dropoffs are a good start for everything. Steep shorelines often have debris from old slips falling in, which gives cover to bullies and koura. Points usually have a reef that holds lots of food for cruising trout and sandy bays are sheltered from lake currents, providing a sheltered home for smelt and bullies. If you are new to a particular lake, the shoreline character will give a good impression of the lakebed character and the time of year and surface water temperature will help you find the thermocline depth. By jigging close to the lakebed at the thermocline depth, you are fishing in the most productive areas. When jigging, the wind will have the final say in where on a lake you fish and whether to drift or anchor. Anchoring can be done in any conditions and locations, with the best being a moderate breeze gently swinging the boat that is anchored over a dropoff, or at the end of a reef so that the boats swing allows you to jig a variety of depths and lakebed. Anchoring in calm conditions allows the use of very light tackle and to accurately target a trout located on the sounder. Jigging from a drifting boat allows a lot of water to be searched. Ideally, drifting at right angles to the shore is best, either into it or away to facilitate jigging in a variety of depths. If a particular depth is producing consistently, go to areas where a drift parallel to the shore or reef is possible. The best drifting conditions are in a breeze that ruffles the water surface and moves the boat at about 1–3km per hour, with or without a sea anchor deployed. When having difficulty keeping on the bottom, it's time to move to a calmer area, or anchor. Before beginning to jig, have a practice drift to check out speed and direction, as well as the lakebed.

The actual physical method of jigging for trout is simple. Drop the chosen rig to the bottom, having picked a weight or jig that is as light as possible but gets it down quickly and is easy to keep down. This is usually from 1–3oz, or 20 to 80 grams. As soon as the lakebed is hit, place the reel into gear and set the flip control. Point the rod tip downwards, keeping the line tight, and give a short smooth flick up, moving the tip about 30cm and then bounce on the lakebed again. Do this several times before winding in two metres of line. As you drift along, give the odd flick and watch the sounder to check depth. If you are drifting into shore, you will feel the weight or jig re-hit the lakebed. Bounce it several times, then re-lift it two metres. Repeat this until the drift is complete.

If you are drifting away from shore, every time your lures are more than two metres off the lakebed drop them, bounce several times, and hold until depth increase again. Bouncing the lakebed not only confirms you are there, but encourages any trout nearby to investigate the vibrations, sound, and skiffs of silt sent out by the weight or jig. Drifting your lures within 2–3m of the bottom means you are in the natural hunting grounds of trout stalking their prey. Interestingly, strikes detected when the weight is bouncing the lakebed are often tentative and require a quick positive strike to hookup. Strikes when lures are drifting 2–3m off the lakebed are solid and secure. If a strike is missed, quickly drop the jig back to the lakebed and slowly reel in about five metres. This technique encourages trout to re-hit the jig or lures. Perhaps it resembles a stunned victim the trout has hit and which it can now devour at leisure. Another productive variation ideal for open water and snag-free lakebed areas is simply dragging and bouncing the weight or jig along the bed as you drift. Point the rod down the line and feel for the bounces as the weight or jig drags along the bed. Watch the sounder for depth changes and, if getting shallower, wind in to reduce snagging. If going deeper or you no longer feel the lakebed, let out line until you do. A long drift with this method can result in a lot of line out.

Another way to use your jig setup is to anchor and cast out and allow the jig setup to drop to the lakebed, then drag it slowly with a bit of action across the bed and back up to the surface. Variations of this include doing the same up or down the face of the dropoffs, which has exciting potential to really catch fish since this is where most of the feeding activity takes place. These techniques can also be employed in the thermocline in open deep water. To help judge the amount of line needed out to fish in the thermocline, mark your line every 10 metres with a waterproof pen.

In summary, we are moving the jig and lures up and down a three metre wide band, encouraging trout to investigate by bouncing the bottom and, with the occasional flick of the rod, giving the lures or jig an exciting visual signal to a following trout. By staying close to the lakebed or within the thermocline, we are placing our lures in the location trout are most frequently hunting food. Jigging enables this to be done more accurately and consistently than other methods. Jigging started as a method to catch trout during the summer when they were forced to stay in deep water and traditional fishing methods could not reach them. But now jigging is practised year round in depths as shallow as five metres. Experienced anglers carry a light rig for shallow waters and a heavier one for the deep stuff and a tackle box of different weights, flies, jigs, and rubber body jigs. Jigging is presently practised mainly in the central North Island lakes, but, typically, Kiwi anglers are more and more experimenting at a wider variety of places around the country. Inevitably, it will be successful everywhere, including with insect copying fly patterns and where regulations allow dead or live baits. Why not use it in large rivers, such as the lower Waikato, or even for salmon in Otago Harbour. One thing is for sure…jigging is a sporting and interesting way for all the family to catch fish and many new jigging innovations will evolve in future.

Fly pattern and jig selection is an important part of jigging success. Future improvements to jig fishing will include the development of more effective jigs and lures. To help develop your own, think about this following strategy, involving light in water.

Light behaves both as a wave and a particle of energy, called photons. Each colour has a different wavelength and amplitude. This determines how deeply each colour can penetrate water. Colours such as blue and violet, with shorter wavelengths and more energy, can be seen deeper than colours such as red and yellow, which have longer wavelengths and less energy. This is further effected by water clarity and turbidity. This means that the fly pattern or jig you have selected will not look the same colour to a trout at a particular depth as it does to you — in fact, it may completely disappear. For example, a red fly or jig deeper than five metres will no longer look red because all the red colour wavelengths cannot penetrate any deeper, so they will effectively disappear and the colour will look completely different. Exciting developments await anglers prepared to experiment with colours and their effectiveness at different depths. The ability to fish with up to three flies or lures makes for some interesting options.

Small Boat Fishing Tactics

BY PETER CHURCH

The trout rose in a lazy contented way, right under the bank where the overhanging bush provided a steady supply of cicadas. The oars were rested quietly in the rowlocks as the boat drifted into casting range. The fish rose again betraying its position and heading. The angle and distance were judged and the cast made to intercept the cruising fish close to the bank. The foam cicada settled on the water for a couple of seconds before being sucked down by the trout. After a delay that seemed to last forever, but is so necessary on stillwater, the hook was set, the rod raised, and at the same time a couple of quick strokes on the oars resulted in the line running clear of the weed and the fish being landed in the deep water. A satisfying result to careful teamwork between angler and boatman in a situation where a shore base approach was impossible.

Using a small boat like this to ambush cruising trout is just one example of the opportunities small boat fishing allows on so many New Zealand waterways.

New Zealanders are boating mad. Look at any of the boat ramps around the major lakes during the holiday period. The family out in the five to six metre multi-purpose runabout for fishing or water sports. From a fishing point of view, it is not necessary to use the big boat. In fact, using a small boat or dinghy can help the fishing. The three to four metre dinghy can allow the fisherman to access many places larger boats can not, and with a lot more stealth and control, which all means better fishing opportunities.

There are other advantages to using the small boat, too. It is easy to launch, so access to fishing spots that do not have a boat ramp is possible. A special vehicle is not needed for towing and an ordinary trailer can be easily converted to carry a small boat.

The type and layout of a particular boat is a personal decision. The problem with using small boats for fishing is where to store all the equipment and still have room to fish. There is nothing worse than working hard to hook a fish and then lose it because the flyline wrapped around a piece of gear lying in the bottom of the boat as the fish ran. Try to keep the deck area clear by using storage lockers and areas under seats or floorboards. If this is not possible, as is the case in many dinghies, use plastic boxes with tops for storage. The idea is to reduce the number of points in the boat to catch lines and to stop movement around the boat. There are some simple solutions. For example, use boxes for seats, or the bailing bucket can become a stripping basket for the flyline.

The small boat is a very versatile fishing tool. Along with trolling, there are a variety of fishing methods for which small boats are particularly suited. Drift fishing and ambush fishing are two methods that take advantage of the characteristics of the small boat.

Drift fishing, or loch style fishing, has been used on the lakes and lochs of Britain for centuries. The aim of this technique is to let the boat drift in a controlled manner with the wind, while the fisherman casts ahead of the moving boat. To control the drift, a drogue or sea anchor is used, holding the boat at right angles to the wind direction and slowing the boat speed so that the fly or lure can be fished effectively. The advantage of this technique is that a lot of water can be covered very quickly and efficiently, meaning more opportunities for fish to see the fly or lure. The small boat is perfect for this method because the low profile catches less wind than a 5m or 6m craft with a cabin. It allows for better control of boat speed and direction.

This technique is good for fishing on smaller lakes, or over areas of shallow water with depths up to six metres. It can work very well over and around weed beds.

Setting up the boat for a drift is easy. Get up wind of the planned fishing area, drop the sea anchor over the upwind side of the boat, and tie it off at each end. Ideally, the boat will drift slowly down wind over the area.

The key to catching fish is to find the depth at which fish are feeding, then keeping the fly or lure working at that level. This means having the right equipment. With flyfishing, this will involve carrying a number of different lines — floating, slow and fast sinking — to cover the different water conditions. When the fish are feeding on the surface — cicada or green beetle time for example — the floating line is naturally the best option. By casting with the wind and letting the boat drift down on the fly, it will fish in a natural way.

The angler will need to control the line by stripping and mending the slack, so the fly does not start dragging, and be ready to strike.

In light wind conditions, a nymph can be fished on a floating line. With this technique, vary the weight of the nymph and the leader length to adjust the depth of the fly, so that it is fishing just over the weed or bottom. Retrieve the line just a little quicker than the boat speed, keeping in touch with the fly and thereby twitching the fly. This can be a very good way of fishing the damsel nymph. Detect the take by feel or use an indicator.

When using a sinking line, set up the boat in the same way and cast downwind. Depending on the type of sinking line and the boat speed, allow the line to sink a little before starting the retrieve. The idea is to have the fly just touching the weed or lake bottom every now and then. It can take some experimentation to get the right combination of line to boat speed to achieve this. The other variable is the rate of retrieve on the fly. Retrieving slowly, just matching the rate of drift, will let the fly sink. By speeding up the rate of retrieve, the fly will lift in the water. In windy conditions, this can be quite an active way of fishing, with the faster boat speed requiring a faster rate of retrieve to keep the fly fishing well.

The take when fishing with the sinking line can feel quite soft because the boat is moving towards the fish when the bite occurs. The trick is to strike on feeling the slightest resistance on the line. There are two hot strike points on the retrieve. The first is as the fly lifts off the bottom, the second as the fly is lifted off the water. It is possible to extend the lift by raising the rod at the end of the retrieve and retrieving the line right up to the start of the leader. The take can be quite visible with fish rushing up from the bottom to grab the fly just centimetres from the side of the boat. There seems to be something about dragging the fly back against the wave action that can really get the fish biting, which makes this form of trout fishing exciting.

The sinking line will work with most wet flies and streamers. Where two flies are allowed, using contrasting patterns can work well — like a Red Setter with a small black Woolly Bugger on the bottom.

This drifting technique will also work with the spinning rod. The same principles apply. Use a bubble to get the necessary casting weight for the dry fly or nymph. With the nymph the bubble will also act as the strike indicator. Using different weighted spinning lures and rates of retrieves, it is possible to fish sub-surface on the drift.

When ambushing or stalking trout, the small boat can be used as a casting platform in a very similar manner to saltwater flats fishing. The low profile and stealth technology oars or paddle, will allow the fisherman to get within casting range of many fish.

This can work well on fish feeding on terrestrials or smelt, for example, where the fish are visibly cruising and it is possible to cast well ahead of the fish to avoid spooking them. This is full on sight fishing with all the normal challenges that casting to trout in clear water present. Good presentation with the right leader and fly is paramount. As most of this type of fishing is in shallow water, a floating line is all that is necessary. The key ingredient is not spooking the fish with the boat, which can be a bit tricky in windy conditions where a bit of rowing muscle may be needed to hold the boat in position. It can be frustrating, with the fish making sudden course changes and swimming under the boat. Another advantage to using the small boat for sight fishing in still water is the ability to manoeuvre the boat into position where the light angle is best for spotting the fish.

Teamwork is important, with the person on the oars needing to judge the distance and direction to the fish for a potential cast to work. Another approach that requires teamwork and a little work on the oars is shotgunning the shoreline. When the light or weather conditions make it impossible to spot fish in the shallows, row parallel to the shoreline at an easy casting distance. Throw the fly tight to the shore and then strip it away from the edge. This is a bass fishing tactic that will work on trout, particularly along swampy shorelines in water up to two metres deep.

Using the small boat, anchored, as a fixed fishing platform is very popular. In essence, the fisherman is allowing the fish to come to him. There are some tactics that can help improve the catch rate.

Always use two anchors to stop the boat from swinging so that the line stays straight in the water during the retrieve. If the boat is swinging, a belly will form in the line, making it difficult to feel the take and fish the fly effectively. As the boat swings, the movement will speed up the line so the retrieve will be faster than the fisherman may want and the fly will lift up in the water column. Get ready to anchor in plenty of time, then anchor for and aft on tight lines. If the situation is suitable, anchoring at right angles to the wind will eliminate any swinging motion. Use chain on the anchor line to help the anchors hold. It can be frustrating to get anchored in the right position and then have the anchors drag in the breeze.

Where to anchor on a lake can be quite daunting if local knowledge is not available. There are some general rules to follow. Look for underwater structure, dropoffs, weed beds, and holes. These are natural feeding places for the fish. Try to anchor so that the fly is fishing from deep water into shallow up the face of the dropoff or weed bed. Another tactic is to anchor so the fly is fished along the dropoff or weed bed, the theory being that the fly will stay in the feeding zone for longer giving more chance for a fish to see the offering.

Using a small boat for anchoring can take some of the stress out of the exercise, in comparison to anchoring a larger craft. Again, the small size can be a real advantage in reducing the silhouette the fish may see.

Using small boats for fishing demands a level of respect for the boat, water, weather, and other water users. There are some very simple rules when operating. Never overload the boat, and always check the weather conditions, safety equipment, and fuel. When moving in the boat, do so slowly and coordinate movements with the other passengers. Landing fish can always be interesting if everybody looks over the side at the same time. The idea is to have a fishing trip, not a swim.

The increasing pressure on many of our river fisheries is forcing anglers in New Zealand to start looking for new and different fishing opportunities. Many of the stillwater fisheries around the country present opportunities to explore and develop some options. Lake fishing can be frustrating. It may take some time and a number of visits to a particular piece of water before the pattern of fish behaviour is worked out and success forthcoming. A little patience can be well rewarded.

A Not Half Bad Way To Fish

BY GLENN MACLEAN

Flyfishing for me is a solitary sport. Well almost . . . the dog is always good company. Any suggestion that my wife Sue might accompany me usually elicits a comment that there are a hundred things she'd rather do than stand bored on the side of some river. Fair enough.

Lake fishing is a different story, however. Come 5.30am on a calm Saturday in spring and most likely Sue, and the dog, will be happily ensconced in the middle of our aluminium dinghy. A dramatic change for someone who lists sleeping in among her favourite hobbies.

Sometimes as keen anglers we become just a little bit ethereal about why we go fishing and amidst all the sentiment about the beauty of the surroundings, or the challenge of a difficult fish, we overlook that for many the thrill simply is catching fish, any fish, any how. When Sue climbs out of bed in the early hours, it's with the expectation she will catch fish, hopefully lots of fish, but nearly always some. The spectacular arrival of the new day will add to the experience, but ultimately she knows she will have fun. That's the essence of harling on Lake Taupo.

Unfortunately for many visitors to the Taupo district, they spend a lot of time on the water watching others have the fun while they miss out. How do you get to share in the smiles?

As the trees around the lake shake off the cold of winter, the willows bursting into bud, the kowhais into glorious yellow, deep within the lake, smelt — the small whitebait-like fish that dominate the diet of Taupo trout — start to feel the urge to spawn. They move out of the depths where they have spent the previous months in vast shoals up onto the sandy shallows around the lake edge. Here in only one to two metres of water they lay their eggs in the fine sand, the eggs hatching 10 to 14 days later depending on the water temperature. The bulk of spawning occurs prior to Christmas, but many fish spawn a second time soon after, so over the whole spring and summer period there are always multitudes of smelt in the shallows. It's hardly surprising that the young trout growing in the lake are attracted to this concentration of their prime food.

But that is only half the story. Coinciding with this is the return of thousands of their older brothers and sisters from the spawning tributaries. Tired and emaciated after months of spawning activity, they ravenously seek food in order to regain physical condition. The huge shoals of smelt in such confined areas along the shore are surely just what the doctor might order. It is this feeding free-for-all that anglers can so effectively exploit by harling.

Harling is simply the trailing of a fly or lure at shallow depth behind a moving boat. I use the term "simply" deliberately because harling is best kept a simple pursuit, done simply. A 3.5m dinghy, the rhythmic chugging of an old Seagull outboard, and some basic tackle will do the job as well or even better than bigger, more sophisticated and more expensive equipment.

My favourite harling rod started out as a five-weight flyrod, which lost its tip in an argument with a car door and subsequently became an ultra light spinning rod. Sue prefers a slighter stiffer boat rod, but just as suitable is the flyrod anglers use to fish the Taupo streams in winter. The only drawback is the extra length, which in a small boat, with several people and even a dog on board, can prove somewhat awkward. Hooked in shallow water without the confinement of a stream bank, the fight on light tackle is strong and explosive. It seems a pity to miss out on this by using rods better suited to landing hapuka.

On each rod is a single action fly reel. Commonly, two sorts of harling lines are used and Sue and I use one of each. The first is a fast sinking flyline, which tends to work best before the sun is in the sky and over the shallower runs. The other is the standard rig used by local fishing guides made from one colour of lead line (10 metres) attached to several hundred metres of monofilament backing. The lead line can be obtained from an old lead line previously used for deep trolling, or purchased from sports shops where it is often sold to provide lead wire for tying weighted nymphs. Overall, this line, which fishes deeper than a sinking flyline, catches more fish for us. One line not commonly used in Taupo, but which many Rotorua anglers possess, is a LED line, which is also ideal. Even though we fish in shallow water, it is still essential to get lures down several metres. For this reason, using straight monofilament is not usually successful except for rare occasions when fish are taking on the surface, or if used in conjunction with diving lures or downriggers.

To the end of the flyline or lead line, I add a trace of five metres of 3.5kg nylon. Some length is necessary to get the lure well back from the boat and several very successful anglers recommend much longer lengths. Up to you. I haven't found it necessary — an extreme example occurring early one morning when a sizable brown took the fly dangling in the water beside me as I waited to complete a turn before putting it back out. It's not a trick I would care to repeat.

The use of flies or lures is a matter of preference. Local guides often use lures, in part because the additional drag on the line makes it easier for clients unfamiliar with the gear to lay the line out. As always, each angler has favourite lures, but there would be few tackle boxes that do not contain some form of Cobra, Tasmanian Devil, or Kiwi lure. Different colours all have their moments, but proven performers include the spotty gold and fluorescent pink variations. Occasionally when the harling gets hard, swapping to a smaller lure only 25mm long can make a difference. Don't overlook the ubiquitous black Toby either, a lure which gets better the more scratched and worn it becomes.

A fly can be used in a variety of ways with a lure and seems to

In the surf after salmon [PHOTO: ROSS MILLICHAMP]

To the victor go the spoils [PHOTO: ROSS MILLICHAMP]

A difficult trout mastered
[PHOTO: ROSS MILLICHAMP]

The tannin-coloured water of the West Coast is home to monster browns

increase the strike rate. One of the more common rigs is to run the fly on a dropper, or slide directly on the mainline a metre above the lure.

I prefer two flies, largely because the pace is much more leisurely and I like that. Traditionally, Taupo harling flies were tied on #4 or #6 hooks, and even occasionally on #2 hooks. Sometimes though, in the calm preamble to another scorcher of a day, swapping to smaller flies tied on #8 hooks is the subtle difference between having a fish to put on the evening barbecue and going home empty-handed.

A smelt in the water is largely translucent, any image dominated by a thin black backbone and the gut cavity. Silicon smelt are very lifelike imitations, but proven patterns such as the Parsons' Glory and Grey Ghost are equally effective. Not that imitation is always necessary.

A Green Orbit is a proven performer early in the season and the Yellow Lady is perhaps the single most used harling fly. Its garish appearance put me off using it for several years, but one day in desperation I tied on one. Rarely since has at least one Yellow Lady not been part of our harling rig. Since it is just as easy to use two flies as one, we normally use a #8 Yellow Lady on each rod and a second fly that is a much more faithful imitation. Put the flies, one on a 150mm dropper, about lm to 1.5m apart. This covers the options and, if we are not having success, I look to alter things such as the depth being fished rather than the flies.

So, having kept the gear simple, how do we use it?

When trout are feeding in the shallows, they feel somewhat vulnerable. Instinctively, they feel visible and exposed. Under the cover of darkness, or on rough, overcast days, they may feel secure enough to remain. But as the day brightens and settles into a flat mirror, most trout slide back into the depths to await the next evening. One of the joys of being on holiday is sleeping in. Unfortunately, arriving at the lake at 7.30am and expecting to catch fish harling are not usually compatible. It is sometimes written that early morning and late evening are equally successful, but as much as that might suit a holiday timetable, it is not usually the case. If you want consistent success, be on the water at first light or soon after, otherwise enjoy the sleep in and bacon and eggs for breakfast.

A drive down the eastern shore in the early morning will reveal suitable areas to prospect. Areas like Five Mile Bay, Hatepe, Motutere, Stump Bay, and Kuratau will be dotted with numerous craft crisscrossing back and forth over the extensive shallows. Launching small craft directly off the beach can access many of these areas.

Edging out into the bay, slowly strip line from the reel, and let it pay out behind the boat. If using lures, first hold the lure on a short line where you can watch its action and adjust boat speed to optimise this. If using flies, imagine walking on the surface of the water (if only) at a leisurely pace beside the boat and set the boat speed so you and the boat do not drift apart. Most mornings we start with about two-thirds of the flyline out, gradually putting it all out as the morning progresses, along with our lead line trailing from 15m of monofilament. Each line has its own sinking characteristic. The more you put out, the deeper it will fish — to a point. It's a matter of trial and error to work out just how much to put out so the flies are in the strike zone.

Hopefully at this point, we get our first strike. Some years ago when working for a very successful Rotorua fishing guide, his big lesson was never to try and slow the initial run. Hold the rod tip up, keep your hand away from the reel, and let the trout go. Over the course of hundreds of clients, there was always an odd one who knew better, or who managed to wrap the reel in the folds of his jersey, or, in the sheer panic of hooking a fish, grabbed the reel. Almost inevitably, the fish would come off. The strike might be explosive, or just a series of tugs. Keep the boat going forward until the fish takes the lure solidly, hold the rod up, cut the motor, and enjoy the scream of the reel. Once the fish stops its initial run, fight the fish relatively hard. Typically, the fight settles down into a series of thrusts and counter thrusts, the fish reluctant to yield the last few metres. If it all goes well, land the fish with a landing net. That's part of the experience. But don't kill needlessly.

Where there is one fish, there usually are others. It is always a good idea to run back through the spot where a fish has just been hooked. The age-old trick of lining up something prominent in the foreground (not another boat) with an object on the horizon to give a bearing helps locate the spot. If you are the only boat, follow whatever track appeals. But if it's crowded, follow the flow, usually by running parallel to the shore. When everyone does this, a number of boats can pass back and forth quite happily. But it only takes one boat running across the flow to sour things. Fish can be anywhere between the shore and the dropoff and on some days they are everywhere. On others, they are in quite localised areas. Running just inside the dropoff often can be a successful ploy when the fishing is hard. Often the fish close to shore are poorer conditioned fish recovering from the rigours of spawning and the best fish are taken nearer the deep water.

The fishing usually comes on as soon as it starts to get light, but occasionally the action doesn't start until the sun touches the water. In full swing, lures are taken as soon as lines are run out and numerous fish will be hooked over a period of an hour or two. Then, all of a sudden it goes quiet and it's over until tomorrow.

Harling, to me, is sitting in the sun on our back deck, listening to the Saturday morning sports show after another successful morning, the aroma of fresh coffee in the air, the leftovers of a fresh fried trout in front of me, and the dog chewing noisily on a fish head on the lawn. It's a different experience to flyfishing on a wilderness stream, but in it's own way, it's not half bad.

Letting Rip At The Rip

BY PETER CHURCH

Rivermouth flyfishing from the stern of a boat can be one of the most entertaining brands of the sport. It is a regular part of the angler's diet in places around the central North Island, but I suspect that in many of the South Island's larger lakes pickings at rivermouths could be quite productive as well. Anywhere where colder water comes into warmer water is a natural congregation point for trout and this is where boat flyfishing is at its best.

In this discussion, I will be dealing primarily with North Island rainbow-based lake fisheries because that is where my experience is most extensive. But there is no reason why what works in the North Island will not work in the South Island, providing it is legal. And that is an important point. Before setting out to fish just any old rivermouth, check local regulations to ensure it is legally fishable by boat. On some southern lakes you can pull up to a rivermouth, park, anchor, and flyfish. On others you cannot and boats simply troll these areas instead.

The thing people struggle with first when rivermouth flyfishing by boat is finding the rip. That sounds ridiculous, but it's true. At times when the lake level is high, or the water is rough, the rip is not easily distinguishable. I find the rip through experience more than anything, but for the average Joe Bloggs there are some giveaways. Telltale signs include:

A]   A difference in water colour

B]   A difference in wave pattern, just like a tidal rip, and

C]   Sometimes the rip can be identified because of debris coming down — sticks and leaves and so on.

On a flat, calm day, there may appear to be no rip, but it is always possible, providing the water is clear, to see debris moving below the surface — if you look carefully.

Having identified the rivermouth and the rip, the next hurdle is knowing precisely where to park the boat. The key position is always the middle of the current. Nine out of 10 times this is the safest bet. The standard rule here is to anchor in the middle of the rip if it's available. If not, the next most favourable positions are those closest to the middle with the edges of the rip being least favourable. The only time this rule changes is when the water is dirty. Then the edges come into play more.

Because rivermouth boat fishing is so popular these days, most times you arrive someone will already be there. In these situations, I tend to go to the side of the rip that shows the strongest flow, working on the theory that where the most current is, the most fish will also be.

If the rip is really crowded, as the main mouth at the Tongariro delta sometimes becomes during holidays, I set up right on the edge. This area is the third most likely alternative for fish.

Knowing how to anchor is essential. Always use two anchors when flyfishing rivermouths, irrespective of the size of the mouth, or the strength of the current. You must stop the boat from swinging. Why? So you don't get a big belly in your flyline when retrieving the fly. But also because it is anti-social to be swinging about on a single anchor if other people are fishing alongside. It doesn't do anyone's temper any good having a boat banging into the side of another.

Never anchor too deep. The general rule: have the back of the boat just over the dropoff. Most fish feed on the dropoff, unless the mouth is really shallow. If it is shallow, anchor further out. But practically speaking, most mouths where an angler uses a boat to fish from will have big dropoffs.

When anchoring, try to keep the anchor lines tight, with one anchor in the shallows and the other in the deep. Pull up tight on the anchor lines as you set up, keeping the boat secure in the middle. Anchoring is made infinitely easier with a 5ft to 6ft length of chain tied to the anchor.

Obviously, conditions dictate when rivermouth flyfishing from a boat is best. Never fish in a full flood, or in extreme winds. Premier conditions are when there is no moon. Also, if fishing for feeding fish, the best time is when the river is coming off a flood and clearing. When fishing for spawning fish, the ideal time is just before flooding. Rivermouth fishing can be productive in quite dirty water, but knowing how dirty is something that only comes through trial and error.

When anchoring, certain laws of etiquette should be followed. Don't anchor so close to another boat that you have to backcast over the top of it. When anchoring next to someone, how close you set up depends on the size of the rip, the casting ability of the anglers on the boat, and the ability of the skipper to anchor up. Remember, it doesn't do anyone any good to have to pull out a fly from the back of a neighbour's head. Most of the time boats can safely and comfortably anchor within 6ft to 10ft of each other. I've seen up to 19 boats safely anchored alongside each other at the Tongariro delta in summer and everyone fishing happily without worries.

Experience has taught me several tips about fishing rips from anchored boats. If you are first into a rip, go quietly so as not to stir up fish. If fishing a rip with others, be aware of what they are doing and avoid tangling lines. Never cast across another's line. Don't run your boat up on the silt at any cost. Silt, particularly ash-laden silt, will destroy water pumps. Boats with large cabins should stay clear of rivermouths. They are hard to fish from and they catch the wind a lot more than smaller craft. When leaving a rip where there are several other boats, pull the front anchor first and pull the boat out of the line with the back anchor.

Casting at a rivermouth is an art form. Most people double haul to get distance, using a high density sinking line. HD lines are preferred mostly and shooting heads are favoured for increased distances. Eight or nine weight rods are best to counteract wind, which seems to be an inevitable curse of rivermouth fishing.

Fish slow and deep, with plenty of patience and a large fly box. Nothing is more certain than you will lose flies. Most importantly, fish your fly all the way up to the surface. Trout will often hit no more than 10ft off the stern.

Stalking South Island Stillwaters

BY LES HILL

The term stalking is now frequently used in flyfishing and high country crystal clear waters enhance this form of angling. Stream and river fishermen must be very active in their pursuit. Trout hold largely in one place and the stalking angler has to stealthily seek each contact, moving from lie to lie or pool to pool.

Along the margins of a pond or lake, an angler's intention is the same — to locate feeding fish. However, often roles can be reversed with angler remaining passive and trout mobile and active.

The reason for this change is the essential difference in feeding habits between stillwater and stream fish. River fish enjoy the luxury of the current bringing food to them. In the relatively still waters of a lake, fish must cruise, explore, and forage and move to food.

This promotes one of the most captivating, exciting styles of hunting. The ambush. A style where the angler, concealed and prepared, awaits a passing fish. Here, "await" implies much patience and cunning and the ability to restrain all movement except swivelling eyes or a slow sideways glance. It implies also an understanding that whenever a trap has been set a trout will invariably take longer to appear — such is the perception of time.

While waiting, an ambush angler has to endure frequent discomfort, restrained in unaccustomed positions. Fifteen years have passed, yet I still recall the pain of angular knots digging into my ribs as I lay prone along a horizontal bough overhanging the shores of Lake Mavora. The lake was more than two metres deep along the shore with trees reaching out from a bank. Casting a fly was impossible. Yet fish cruised below, passing frequently — tempting.

My ambush technique was to lie atop a broad bough, concealed from below, with arms outstretched and rod held along the branch, also hidden. I planned to lower a nymph to the lake bed, leaving it settled until a trout approached and then hopefully a small twitch of the line would lift the lure and attract a fish.

I observed life below for a considerable time. It appeared two fish patrolled this shore, keeping a respectful distance from each other yet feeding from the same territory. I waited until both had disappeared, then slid awkwardly head first along the bark and finally came to rest gripping the log desperately with both thighs and one elbow. I peeped over into the water wondering at the worth of my actions.

Committed, I somehow eased several metres of line out and dropped it. The nymph sank, and then came to rest, clearly visible in the clear water. I continued to hold the bough with my left elbow. My right hand gripped the rod, held it against the tree, and my index finger secured the line ready for the twitch and strike.

The larger of the two fish came into view first, nosing the bed, inspecting every stone closely, gathering occasional unseen morsels. As it approached my offering, I lifted the rod tip a fraction. The nymph followed. The fish dived towards the nymph, but stopped short, then continued past more purposely now. Then it circled back for a second look and disappeared in alarm. I waited again.

Some time later, the second trout turned, foraging also. When a metre separated fish and nymph, I lifted the rod again — a little more this time, slowly and gradually — hoping the nymph would imitate an escaping insect. The fish shot forward and engulfed the bait, then sped away as it was stung by the hook.

One cannot land a trout while wrapped around a log by three limbs and holding a rod out with the fourth. I had to return to shore and realistically needed two free hands. What should I do with the rod?

After its initial run the fish came to rest. I flung my rod into the water beside the shore and left the battle to continue without me, while I eased back to the safety of land. Fortunately, the tackle was not towed into the lake and I retrieved all and ended the fight.

Ambushing fish is only one of the excitements that await stalking anglers employing a variety of techniques around the lake shores. The variety equals that offered on rivers and streams.

The South Island contains a wealth of lakes and a surprising variety of stillwaters, which can be grouped by nature and location. Beginning in the north lie the Nelson Lakes, Rotoiti, and Rotoroa. These lakes not only offer challenging fishing, but also lie amidst beautiful, mountains rising to more than 2000 metres. Testimony to the beauty of the area is the fact that its uniqueness has been preserved as a national park.

On a journey down the West Coast, one encounters numerous lakes, smaller than the Nelson pair, and largely less accessible with thick native overhanging most shores. The West Coast lakes are often protected by swampy margins and characterised by their brackish waters. However, for an angler who does not equate success with a large number of fish landed, great sport awaits.

The best-known lakes of the South Island are the Southern Lakes. These stretch from the relative giants of Manapouri and Te Anau in the south to Hawea in central west Otago. Most have some accessible shores, largely along their eastern sides, and are fed from very high rainfall on high fringing mountains. They contain both browns and rainbows and some landlocked salmon. The broad shallows, particularly around some rivermouths, are exciting to fish, such as the mouth of the Eglinton River, or where the Matukituki and Makarora rivers meet Lake Wanaka. Some of the lake outlets are equally productive, such as the outlet from Wanaka.

Along the East Coast are a small number of estuarine lakes with a character of their own. Trout of 10–12lb are not uncommon in both Waituna Lagoon and Lake Ellesmere. However, being on the coast and unprotected by high mountains, squally conditions often prevail.

The inland Otago and Canterbury lakes probably have the best reputation for fishing. Within the provinces are a great variety of waters, from the larger hydro lakes such as Dunstan and Benmore and the neighbouring Ohau, Pukaki, Tekapo group, to Coleridge and Sumner further north. And there are scores of smaller lakes throughout the foothills. Some hold small numbers of large, wary trout, while others, like Lake Lyndon, hold many small fish.

These inland lakes are largely accessible on all shores that are clothed by grass and tussock. They share an openness and exposure to winds from all directions, but the northwesterly in particular can be strong and persistent.

On lake edges an angler can either stalk actively, or wait in ambush for trout to move into view.

Close to stream mouths or a deeper channel cutting into the shore, several fish will often feed. A patient ambush in such a place may be the most discreet successful method.

Where trout are more widely dispersed, with large territories, one may wait for a considerable time for a fish to pass. It may prove more productive to cautiously seek the fish, giving great attention to hot spots, such as deep water shelves, weed beds, inlets, obstructions, and variations in the lake bed. Watch, too, for finning fish or telltale dimples.

While not always the most successful, the dry fly is for many the most exciting way to catch a lake trout. I try a dry first on many fish, either placing it well ahead of the fish and waiting for it to move onto the fly, or from a side-on or front position I may drop the fly just inside the fish's area of vision — about a metre or two. If done delicately, the dropping fly will be noticed.

Using a dry fly with a nymph in tandem may have many advantages, depending on circumstances. Using a floating fly with a tiny nymph in or on the surface film — Green Beetle with a Midge Pupa — covers two options for surface feeding trout. The dry fly, being tied within a metre of the tiny nymph, indicates where the nymph is and warns of a take. In windy conditions, a dry fly serves even better as an indicator, while having the advantage of being engulfed itself on occasions.

While nymphs may be fished with a dry, they are normally fished alone and may be employed in several ways. An angler may keep the nymph active, imitating a free-swimming form, such as a waterboatman or damselfly, or the imitation may be left inert in the surface film as food trapped there. The nymph may be allowed to sink to the lake bed and then gently lifted as a trout passes. Sometimes a lightly weighted nymph landed close to a cruising fish is often taken as it sinks.

The appeal of lake fishing is easily explained. Rivers run confined like narrow ribbons through the hills, across the plains, often shaded, disciplined. Lakes lie open — to the rain, wind, sun, sky, to the eye. Sometimes tranquil, mirror-like, inviting. Sometimes whipped by squalls into a fury. Small waters may freeze solid, be blanketed in snow, then months later be uncomfortably warm in the shallows for sensitive inhabitants.

Lakes — the eccentric waters. And they harbour trout. What more could we desire?